HEAVEN'S MESSENGER

HEAVEN'S MESSENGER

Dennis Binks

HEAVEN'S MESSENGER

Heaven's Messenger

Text Copyright © Dennis Binks 2017

Dennis Binks has asserted his right in accordance with the Copyright Designs and Patents Act 1988 to be identified as the author of this work.

All rights reserved

No part of this publication may be lent, resold, hired out or reproduced in any form or by any means without prior written permission from the author and publisher. All rights reserved.
Copyright © 3P Publishing Ltd

First published in 2017 in the UK

Set in Giovanni 12pt

3P Publishing Ltd
C E C, London Road
Corby
NN17 5EU

A catalogue number for this book is available from the British Library

ISBN 978-1-911559-26-9

Cover design: Jamie Rae

People who inspired me to write this:

Mum, now in Spirit, Nanna, Dad, Lee, my wife Evelyn, Anne, Hayley, Natasha and Craig.

Contents:

Foreword	7
Liverpool	9
Nanna	14
Early pickings	19
Slowly developing	27
Ta ta Liverpool	33
Being different	42
Early love	50
Sergeant's exam	56
All change at home	61
Unified Fighting Systems	77
Lee	84
New Year's Day	91
Bump in the night	102
You're Roman Catholic now	113
Evidence	120
Dad. It's me	125
Lynn	130
Elmer Street	138
Stansted	144
Denmark	152
Britain's Psychic Challenge	157
Mum	172
Final thoughts	180

Foreword:

If after all this I gave love and light to one person, if just one person really knew their loved ones were alive and well due to the work I do, then it was all worth it.

I believe that if you know someone's story then you can understand that person more. I want you to know that we all have challenges to face and to make your spirit stronger these obstacles are not always easy and painless.

Dennis Binks – Corby – June 2017

HEAVEN'S MESSENGER

CHAPTER 1 - Liverpool

I suppose I was a typical Liverpudlian lad. I lived in Carrasbrook Road, Walton with my mother, Audrey, father, William and my sister, Stella.

I remember very well my father leaving for work on his bike when he did his rounds. He was a collector for the provy, or the Provident, and he was a big guy with a short fuse.

One day while at the dinner table Mum said, "I can't find Morse's payment card." Morse was like the provy or Provident, you had things and paid later for them.

Dad replied, "Surely we are finished paying that love?" Mum just shrugged and handed Dad the payment card, he looked at it and said, "We finished paying what we owe about six months ago. You mean to tell me this man's still calling and collecting money from us?"

Mum just stood there and said, "Well yes."

The next Tuesday evening Dad should have been out collecting, but he stayed in and waited. Sure enough at eight o'clock there was a knock at the door and through the letter box a man shouted, "Morse and Co." Dad said, "Leave it to me love."

Mum nodded. Dad opened the door and the man said, "Hello. Morse and Co." The man was very self-assured and looked quite smug. Dad looked him up and down. I must say that Dad was about five foot ten but was built like a battle ship. He had huge arms.

Dad said, "What do you want whack?" (Whack being a Liverpool term for friend or mate). The man opened his folder and looked nervous, as me and Stella watched from the front bedroom window. "Errr, I have called to collect."

Dad said, "Oh yeah? How much do we owe like?" Again, the man looked worried and fidgeted, he opened his folder and said, "Only two more payments. Are you Mr Binks?"

"No. I am the one that's going to knock your teeth out!" Dad replied and head butted the man who staggered back, folder and papers flying all over the front of the house. The man fell against the front gate and Dad got the man's head in a head lock as he was bending over and trying to breath. Dad opened the front gate and placed his head between the gate and the gate post and began slamming the gate on his head.

I remember blood everywhere and I jumped from the window, shocked and upset at what I had seen. I was five years of age, a very skinny, pale faced lad. Dad walked in, his hands covered in blood, "Well, he won't bloody well be back girl," he said to Mum.

I looked out the window and there, lying unconscious in our front yard, was the man lying on his back, blood all over his face and head. I backed away slowly, I felt really sick. Stella put her arm around me and cuddled me, "Don't think about it Dennis, okay? Look at me, he will be okay."

I just nodded.

Dad had a bad temper, and you knew when he was losing it because his face would go livid white, but at the same time, to us kids, he was loving and we always felt safe with him. He never hit any of us.

Me, aged three, with sister, Stella, rear left

One day my sister Stella came home from school, we all sat at the table for dinner when my dad noticed Stella had a black line in a square shape around her mouth.

He stopped eating, leaned forward staring for a couple of seconds and then said, "What the hell's that around your mouth girl?"

Stella put her hand to her mouth quickly, suddenly realising it was still there, "Oh! I was talking in class and Miss Edmunds put sticky tape over my mouth."

Dad sat staring for a minute; we all sat silent wondering if Stella was going to be told off for getting into trouble, but Dad just carried on eating.

Dad was also a lorry driver on odd days. He drove a huge haulage truck and I used to go with him during school holidays.

The following day I was at school when I heard a familiar noise. I was in an upstairs class and, looking out of the window, I saw Dad's truck. I leaned forward to get a better look and I could see Dad climb out with a huge roll of brown packing tape.

He strode straight into school and after about a minute the whole class became quiet as we could hear shouting and a woman screaming. Suddenly, through the glass of the class room door, Miss Edmunds came flying past looking like something from a mummy film. She was covered in brown tape, it was wrapped around and around her, behind ran my Dad screaming, "Don't you ever,

ever, do that to my children again."

Miss Edmunds had six weeks off school to recover. I became aware many years later that the school did not take any action due to what she had done to Stella.

She was very nice to us after that, but I can honestly say we did not take advantage of the fact she was too terrified to even look at us. We sat quietly and always paid attention during the lessons.

CHAPTER 2 - Nanna

Living with us was my grandmother Hilda. She spoke differently to us, very posh, and always went on about how to bring us up which usually started a row between her and my dad. "He was never good enough for you, our Audrey; didn't even know what a sprout was when you met him," Nanna would say.

Nanna used to take us for a meal once a week to a very posh hotel.

I hated this as Nanna would clean and prune my nails with a nail file, "Got to show the half moon," she would say as she pushed the quick back on my finger nails.

My hair was washed and combed with a strict parting. I wore a blazer and short grey trousers and a brilliantly whiter than white shirt and tie. My shoes I had to polish.

Stella was treated the same, her hair immaculate with a huge bow in it, a dress and short white socks.

Nanna wore a hat of hats, with either a dead animal on it or a bundle of feathers. A figure hugging suit, fox furs round her neck and always a long thin cigarette holder and a cigarette, which she held up in the air.

We caught a taxi to the Alicia Hotel near Sefton Park. Nanna would walk in, head up in the air, me and Stella running behind her. Stella would whisper, "She thinks she's Gloria Swanson, Dennis." I remember we had just seen a film starring her, it was called *Rebel Without a Cause.* I was trying to keep up with Nanna and giggling.

In those days in top class hotels the head waiter would meet us at a small table, "Good afternoon Mrs Collins, what beautiful children. Your table is waiting."

In a black suit with tails he looked like a penguin, and as he walked he looked like he was floating to a table in the packed dining room. Of course, in those days, smoking was allowed everywhere. Nanna would walk through the dining room, head back, plumes of smoke everywhere behind her, and wait for the head waiter to pull her seat out and ours.

Once seated we would sit and not talk, no elbows on the table, no picking our noses, and no staring at people eating. We already knew what all the knives and forks were for as Nanna had taken us through every conceivable type of knife, fork and spoon.

"Do not slurp your soup Dennis, tip the bowl towards you boy." Nanna would glare at me, enough to make me want to slither under the table.

But no matter how much she called my Dad, and Nanna would say some terrible things, I loved my Dad, and my Mum.

Nanna

My dad had a real sense of humour. He had a 35mm projector and every Christmas the highlight was all of us huddled together, in the front room, by the flickering coal fire. Dad put a sheet up on the wall, click would go the lights as he switched them off and with the whirl of the projector we would see black and white cartoons of Popeye the Sailor Man and Mickey Mouse.

These where great times. We always had a real, huge coal fire in every room in the house as it was so large.

One day my Dad danced around the room yelling, "We're rich, we're rich."

HEAVEN'S MESSENGER

We all stood in a huddle looking at Dad jumping up and down and holding a brown envelope and some paper in his hand, he bent down and with a huge manic grin on his face he held me on the shoulder and said, "Dennis boy, we are rich beyond our wildest dreams. We won the pools."

In those days, there were pools coupons. There were Littlewoods, Zetas and Vernon's. Dad had scooped the biggest one. Littlewoods.

Dad had to go to work and placed the brown envelope and the coupon behind a porcelain swan on the mantelpiece saying to Mum, "Now Audrey please will you post that and make sure you put a stamp on it?"

Mum nodded, not really perturbed by all the commotion as she was brushing the floors. The day went on as usual and I went to school with Stella.

In the evening, I remember playing with my toys in the living room; it was the warmest room in the house and you could smell that heavy coal smell.

Dad came in from work, he was whistling and smiling, "Hello Dennis, my boy," he said as he picked me up and carried me into the kitchen, "Well Audrey did you post the pools coupon for me? I see its gone." "Gone?" She whispered and hardly moving a muscle, with a dishcloth in her hand and wearing a pinnie, she slowly walked into the living room from the kitchen.

All you could hear was the crackle of the coal fire as I was slowly lowered to the floor. Mum just stood there staring at the mantelpiece, and then with a sigh she said, "I cleaned up the fire place and may have thrown it into the fire."

It was like forever before anyone spoke.

Dad just turned and walked to the bottom of the stairs, I could hear him crying as he slowly climbed the stairs.

Next day it was business as usual, it was breakfast time and me and Stella where getting ready for school. I ran into the kitchen and found Mum and Dad cuddling and kissing, so I ran back out again but happy as Larry that love was in the house again.

CHAPTER 3 - Early pickings

Grandmother who we called Nanna, was a very proficient Clairvoyant Medium and a Psychic. She always knew what we had done, what we were going to do, or even thinking about.

It was mainly women who came for readings from Nanna. We lived in a huge Georgian style house with loads of rooms; it was massive.

Sometimes coming home from school I would notice a lamp in the front room lit, and if there was a red chiffon scarf draped over the lamp giving a red glow, that meant that Nanna was doing readings. I hated this as I was aware there would be a dozen or so women all wearing wrap around pinnies and a scarf tied around their heads, with two pieces of hair sticking out the front of their heads, like Hilda Ogden in *Coronation Street.*

When I opened the front door to the very long hallway, there, sat in about a dozen hard back chairs, the women sat. "Ah there is her grandson, isn't he cute?"

I used to take a deep breath and run, trying to get to the far end of the hall and into the dining room where mother would be, but alas, they would

catch me, ruffle my hair and pinch my cheeks.
I would burst into the dining room with my hat on one side, my jacket half undone, and a dozen or more mint imperials or humbugs in my hand, "I hate that Mum. I hate running through those women."
"Oh Dennis, they think you're cute. Nanna loves doing her readings, so be a good boy and help me with the potatoes, okay?"
Mum would smile and I was fine.
We had to go down some steps to the kitchen, it was a huge kitchen with red tiles on the floor and a large farmers' wooden table in the middle. It was always warm in there and smelt of cooking, and there was a huge black range to cook on. I would stand on a chair and help Mum peel potatoes: "Dennis not big chunks, like this," and Mum would show me again, "Peel it thin, okay?"
These where happy days, I loved these days.

Again, it was a Saturday and I would be with Dad on his bike.
He would tie a cushion on the cross bar and I would sit on this and hold on for dear life and then we would be off, 'WOOOSH' the wind in my face. I would lean back against Dad's chest and hold on. I had never gone so fast in my life, my hair blasting back and my eyes squinting.
I loved this and the different people we would meet. No matter where we went if we passed a milkman with the clinking of his bottles the

milkman would wave and shout, "Hi Bill!" And as we flew past on the bike Dad would wave, or a dustman in the street with a bin on his shoulder, Dad would ring his bell and shout, "Hi Tiny!" And the bin man would shout back to Dad. Everyone knew my dad.

One day we went to a lady's house; Dad knocked the door and shouted, "Only the Provy Love." The lady came to the door, she was about fifty years of age. A big lady about five foot ten inches tall with a lot of wavy hair, which thinking back now, looked like a wig. Behind her was a brown dog, with what looked like a lion's mane.

I said, "Hey Dad look, that dogs got a mane." The lady said, "Oh bless him, it's a Chow lad." The dog came forward and I stroked his head.

 "Both of you come on in, while I find the card." Dad followed her into the kitchen where her card was, and I followed the dog into the front room.

 Many homes had coal fires in those days and sitting in a chair was a very elderly gentleman, he was sitting on the edge of the seat, with his arms out stretched warming his hands by the fire. He was wearing just a vest, trousers, with the braces dangling down, and a pair of tartan slippers. He was thin on top with white sparse hair, his bottom teeth were rotten and under the vest there was a tattoo that had become blurry with age. He smiled, and the dog went and sat next to him. He leaned over the side of the arm chair and began stroking the dog, he said, "London here is a lovely dog, isn't he?"

"Yes, he is. I love his mane. Is that his name, London?" I replied, smiling to myself at such a funny name for a dog.

The man said: "Yes. He was my brother's dog in London, he had him as a puppy but they moved him out and he could not look after him, so we had him, and named him London."

Just then I heard Dad call, "Dennis?"

I said "Ta-Ta," to the man and joined my Dad in the hallway. Dad said, laughing, "Come on now our Dennis."

As I was leaving I said, "Goodbye London."

The lady looked perplexed at me, "How did you know his name was London?"

"The old man sitting in there told me," I replied.

The lady stepped backwards as if she was ready to faint and said, "What did he look like?" She opened the door again and beckoned me in, as I entered there was no one there.

"He was very old, had rotten teeth down there," pointing to my lower teeth, "and was bald. Oh, and he had a vest on with braces down here, and a tattoo on his chest," I replied.

The lady took a hanky from under her sleeve and wiped her nose and eyes. "That was my Dad, Harry," she said to my dad. My dad sat there, knowing what I had seen and the information I had given.

The lady then smiled and said, "What else did he say?" I related about his brother and the puppy;

the lady went to a cupboard and returned with a stick of rock and a photograph in a frame. She showed me the photograph with about twenty odd people in it, all standing in a row. They were all wearing blue blazers and grey trousers and carrying various musical instruments. They all looked about thirty to forty years of age. "Point to him sweetheart if you can see him there," she said. Straight away I pointed to a man wearing a blazer, which had a badge on the breast pocket and a tie.

The lady looked deep at the picture and said, "Ah that is my dad all right, at a reunion with his old Army buddies, a lot younger then, but you got it right lad." She then handed me the rock and as we left she was still sitting, smiling at the picture.

I used to have a recurring dream. It was always very similar. I would suddenly find myself in a wilderness, either in some kind of desert, or in a forest or jungle. I would be scared as I did not know where I was. I would run and run, and sometimes I would wake up with my mum, nanna, or sister saying, "Come on now Dennis, it's only a dream."

I would wake up crying and upset, obviously calling out in my sleep and waking everyone up. But now and then, I would not wake up; there would be a very old and 'knowing' man that would appear, and just say, "This way son." And he would take my hand. The next thing I would wake up as normal in the morning.

As time went on, the dream became less and less but I was later to recognise this man was my Spirit Guide.

I can recall Mr Robson who lived next door, he had a fantastic voice and we would sit and listen to Mr Robson sing, as all my family gathered around the piano in the living room. Nanna would play and Mr Robson would sing. One day as the kitchen was full of people all singing and Nanna playing the piano, I went upstairs to the bathroom and got us two drinks of water, as we could not get to the sink or our bottles of pop, which were Vimto or Sasperella.

I was coming down the stairs with the drinks in my hand when a lady who was climbing up the stairs smiled at me, she was very old and wore a wraparound dress and had hardly any hair on top. It was very thin and you could see her pink scalp, she had just a tuft in the front and she also had a red mark on her forehead.

And then in front of my eyes she just vanished. I ran into the room where everyone was singing and I explained to my mum about the strange lady in our home, saying, "I passed her on the stairs, she looked very pink, and was nearly bald, she had a red mark on her forehead."

Pointing to my forehead, Mrs Robson said, "Did she have just a tuft of hair on top?" And Mrs Robson held up some hair on top showing me, I looked and nodded my head, that was exactly how

her hair was I said.
Mrs Robson ran outside to the telephone box across the road, as we did not have a telephone in those days, neither did the Robson's. After about ten minutes she returned, she looked upset and shocked, she just walked up to Mr Robson and said, "My mother died ten minutes ago, she was suffering terribly with a tumour in her brain that could not be removed."

This was nothing new to me, I had seen Mr Moss after he died.
He was also another good friend of Grandmother's: an old man about seventy years of age who always wore a dark brown suit and a wide brimmed trilby, and a waistcoat with a chain going across the two pockets. He had a huge red nose, and I used to say to Stella, "Here's Rudolph," and she would giggle.
Nanna would call in sometimes to see if he was okay and as he lived nearby he always used to visit us, and every time he would put his hand in his pocket and bring out some pear drop sweets for me and Stella. One day Nanna went to call on Mr Moss to make sure he was well, and she found him sitting in the living room passed away.
Me and Stella didn't go to the funeral, Mrs Robson looked after us. While at Mrs Robson's I wanted some toys, you know what kids are like, they must have that certain toy and nothing else will do, so I ran next door to our home.

I went to my bedroom and as I was coming down the stairs I heard someone coughing, it was coming from our living room. I wasn't really scared as I was expecting to see someone that perhaps had not attended the funeral.

I walked into the room and there was Mr Moss sitting in an arm chair just lighting a cigar, he looked up through the smoke, smiled, and said, "Rudolph ay, here tell your grandmother she has to have this." From his inside pocket, he took a long gold chain with what looked like a small fir cone on the end in gold.

And then he was gone, just like that.

I turned around looking round the room, then ran next door to tell Mrs Robson, who smiled and said, "It is a young mind playing tricks, I am not surprised," looking up at the ceiling as she walked away.

When all the family came home I explained to my mother and Nanna what had happened, Nanna said, "I don't know what he could have meant, I did not want anything from him and I never got anything." And that was that.

CHAPTER 4 – Slowly Developing

Dad was a drummer in a band, I loved to see him practice. "Let me have a go Dad," I would shout and he let me sit behind his huge drum set, and I would play at playing the drums. "No," Dad would say, "Do the Mummy-Daddy first; that is how you learn." Tap tap, tap tap. "Okay Dennis, tap tap, tap tap, Mummy Daddy, Mummy Daddy," Dad said. I tried, but as with a lot of children if I had not learnt it in a week then I had given up.

Dad used to do the odd gig now and then and he would get home about one or two in the morning. He never drank, but one night, I was asleep in bed when I heard shouting. I opened my bedroom door and saw Stella standing at the top of the stairs, listening. I joined her in the dark at the top of the stairs looking down to the lighted hallway. We could hear Dad and unable to understand what he was saying we crept down together, with Stella hugging me saying, "Shhhhh!"

We moved along the hallway to the dining room and peeped in; they were in the kitchen. At that moment, Dad hit Mum, and threw all the Wedgwood crockery at her from the Welsh dresser.

It all smashed on the floor, and one piece cut Mum's heel open, Dad suddenly turned around, his face bright red and eyes glaring with hate. We moved back just in time. He had not seen us.

Dad staggered past us, mumbling, and went upstairs. We shot into the kitchen to Mum "Watch your feet, stand still," Mum said. Stella and I were crying. "I am okay, honest." Mum smiled and picked me up. Limping, she took us into the dining room, Stella went to a drawer and fetched a bandage and a sweeping brush. She made her way to the sink and came back with a flannel, warm water and a towel. I was shocked and very upset. I remember my stomach churning.

"I thought Dad loved you," I said to Mum. "He does love but he has been drinking whiskey. He should never drink that; it sends him nuts," she replied.

Stella began washing Mum's heel, it was a deep cut. "I'll be okay, I'll do that," Mum said and began to wash, dry and bandage the cut.

The next morning was a Saturday, and Dad came down as if nothing had happened. We sat in the dining room for breakfast, then he turned to us and said, "I promise you all I will never drink again." And from that day until he passed to the spirit he never did.

I had always known things about people. One day when I was about six years of age, Mrs Rose, a friend of my mum's, called, leaving her bicycle against the front window.

As she was going I said, "Watch your bike Mrs Rose." She frowned a little, looking puzzled, smiled and said, "Don't worry Dennis, I will." And she rode off smiling.

An hour later she returned, "My bikes gone!" she said. Mum looked at me, and I just shrugged, "I know," I replied.

Another time, Mrs Sinnet, another friend of my mother, came around with her son Stanley. He was the same age as me and we got on okay. As we were playing with some toy cars out the front of my house, I suddenly said, "She is not your mum, is she?"

Stanley looked up from playing and said with a broad Liverpudlian accent like mine, "What do you mean? Of course, she is me mum."

"No, she's not. You have another Mummy."

He laughed and we went on playing. They left soon after, but a day later I came home from school and in the dining room was Mrs Sinnet, sitting drinking a cup of tea with my mum. Mum said to me, "Come here love sit down our Dennis. I want you to think now about yesterday and what you and Stanley spoke about. Did you tell Stanley anything when you were out front playing yesterday after school?"

I sat and thought. "No," I replied, placing my satchel on the hat peg in the hallway. Mum then said, "Come here Dennis, think now love this is important, did you say anything else to Stanley?"

I suddenly turned around and faced Mum, "Oh yeah I remember, I told Stan that you," pointing to Mrs Stanley "wasn't his real Mum."

Mum turned to Mrs Sinnet and said, "Okay I will deal with this."

At that Mrs Sinnet stood up and left.

"Come here our Dennis lad. Don't worry you have done nothing wrong." I sat on Mum's knee, and she said, "You will know things sweetheart, okay? But you cannot always tell people everything. One day you will but for now it is important you know that okay?"

I was puzzled, "Well she's not his mum, is she?"

Mum smiled and said, "No love she is not, Stanley was adopted, but he didn't know. His mummy was going to tell him when he got older."

I just shrugged my shoulders and Mum kissed me on the cheek, "One day young man you're going to be an amazing Medium."

I knew what that was, as every Sunday afternoon Nanna and Mum would hold a development circle in the front room.

At the end of this, if I was home, Nanna would fetch me in. I would stand in the circle with all the circle members sitting on chairs: "Okay Dennis, who do you want to talk to first?"

I would slowly turn and point to someone, maybe a man. I remember that Nanna had the ability to be able to move in on the link, or to understand what the message from the Spirit was. "I want to talk to this man. I have a woman who is holding a rose and she is saying, 'feed the rose.'"

At that moment, wack! I had a stinging pain in the back of my hand. Nanna had just hit the back of my hand with a twelve-inch ruler,

"How dare you interfere with a message from Spirit. That is not what was said. Is it? Is it?"

I just held my hand and began to cry. "I don't know," I blubbered.

"It was," Nanna said, "the lady is holding a rose to you and is saying water the rose."

The man sat back and said, "My God that is Shirley, my sister. I planted a rose on her grave and only yesterday I said to my wife I must water her rose tree. I planted it on her grave, there is only one rose out now."

"Go to your room, and stay there," Nanna said, so I did.

One day there was a knock at the door and a lady about fifty years of age stood there. Mum asked her in. We were all in the living room, Nanna was playing Gin rummy with Dad and some friends.

Mum said, "This lady wants you Mum." Nanna stood up and said, "Hello can I help you?"

The lady replied, "Ellis Moss was my father, I believe you used to call in regular to see if he was okay? And you were the one who actually found him?"

Nanna looked awkward and said, "Well I don't know about look after him, I used to do a bit of shopping for him. He was one of the old school, you know, a gentleman."

The lady smiled and from her pocket pulled out a gold chain with a small gold piece on the end.

I could not quite make it out. Nanna took it and the lady said, "Dad wanted you to have this. It's not much but please take it."

Nanna held it, turned to me just staring at me for a minute, then I recognised it, it was the necklace Mr Moss had shown me in this very living room.

"Thank you my dear. I would love to." With that the lady left.

Nanna knelt beside me, "My, my I don't know what to make of you Dennis, this was amazing son."

I just shrugged and carried on playing with my toys.

I used to wake up during these years when I was around six or seven years of age and it was always between three and four o'clock in the morning.

I would hear people whispering in the dark. I could not make out what they were saying, it was always just out of ear shot.

I would run to Mum and Dad's room, "I am hearing them again Mum." Mum would pull back the sheets and blanket to let me climb in with her and Dad and sleepily she would say, "Okay sweetheart. Don't worry, get in here."

CHAPTER 5 - Ta Ta Liverpool

My dad sometimes worked behind the bar in pubs, and he was asked to take over the running of the NUPSO club. This was a part of Walton Prison where police and prison officers used to drink.

My Dad loved it, and sometimes Mum would help too when they were busy. One day my Mum's sister, Iris, wrote a letter to Mum telling her that where she lived in Rushden, Northants, there was a club where they required a steward and a spouse. Well, they got the job and soon we were on a train leaving Liverpool behind. My mum hated Liverpool and swore one day to get us out.

The pub was called the West End club and we lived in a cottage nearby called Orchard Place.

The town was always full of American airmen as the big American air base, Chelveston, was nearby. The West End club too was always full of Americans.

Dad had been used to handling pubs and clubs in Liverpool. One night the local lads, many of them 'Teddy boys,' were a bit peeved at all the girls in the club hanging around with the 'Yanks', as they were known.

Suddenly a fight broke out and chairs and tables were flying everywhere. Dad jumped over the bar with a pick axe handle and very soon, after some sickening crunches, it was all over.

However, at the next committee meeting Dad was called into the meeting. My dad's first name was Bill. "Bill, we are worried about what happened on Saturday. We have had numerous complaints as to your use of a weapon to stop fights."

My Dad sat there for a minute and replied, "Yes, I did as there were no committee men around to help. I hear they are coming back Saturday as well, if any one of you want to come here and help me, I wouldn't need to protect the property or my family, would I?"

Members of the committee slid low in their seats in case they were asked to show up on Saturday night.

"What, no takers? Oh, I see, you want me on my own to handle this, but with no help, and then complain when I do? Well I want help. This is not going to go away, and I hear this is why the last steward left."

The President of the club coughed, "Errr, we will discuss what you say Bill.

"So, I keep my stick then," Dad replied and got up and walked out.

And he did keep his stick. It was nothing to see Dad and a couple of male bar staff dive in with pick axe handles.

About now my brother Barry was born. I was eight

years of age then.

My Mum had entered a singing competition at the Waverley Hotel in Coffee Tavern Lane, just off the High Street in Rushden.

I remember sitting at the back with Nanna and Stella, and Mum was called on stage. She looked stunning in her new dress and hair all done up.

I had just got over a really bad bout of tonsillitis. Mum stood there, waved her hand in my direction and said, "I would like to sing this song for my son."

Everyone looked round at me, I had tears in my eyes and felt so embarrassed. I mean lads don't cry, do they?

Mum began to sing, *If you love me.* She sang amazingly, people stood up whistling, shouting, and I was standing on my chair screaming at the top of my voice.

My mum would sing this song again for me, but it was to be many years later.

Soon Nanna joined us in Rushden, and once more people were amazed by her Mediumistic abilities. And again, a development circle began.

Nanna ran away from home when she was only fifteen, her mother and father were Irish. Her mother, my great grandmother, was also a Medium, and my great, great grandmother was an Irish Romany living in one of those beautiful wooden caravans that are horse drawn. I still have my great, great grandmother's crystal ball, handed to me by my mother.

Nanna ran away to join a dance troupe in London. Her father came and took her home but again she ran away at only fifteen years of age and joined another dance troupe.

Five times my great, great grandfather took her home, the sixth time he didn't.

Nanna was in one of the dance troupes in London known as the Toppers and was on stage with famous stars of the day.

Violet Carson of *Coronation Street* fame, Anne Shelton and Gracie Fields both singers, and for a long time toured England with two brothers: Charlie and Sid Chaplin.

All the stars of the day would run to her dressing room for readings, "You're going to America Charlie," she said.

"Not likely Hilda," Charlie said, smiling.

"Well you wait and see."

This was well before the time where Charlie and Sid split up and Charlie left for America and became the famed 'Tramp.'

Life went on in Rushden and I met a great pal named Peter Harrison. We had the same sense of humour and we went everywhere together. Him, his younger brother Andrew, me and my brother Barry were inseparable.

I remember coming down stairs one day and Peter was sitting in the living room waiting for me. As I walked in the door, I could hear Nanna talking. When I went into the living room Peter sat there wide eyed and Nanna was talking to an empty chair.

Outside Peter said, "Who was she talking to Dennis?"

I had to explain that Nanna was a Medium and at times would talk to Spirits.

"Wow cool," Peter said and it wasn't ever mentioned again.

Peter and me where at my house during the school holidays when I found my dad's rolling tobacco and papers.

I used to roll the cigarettes and sell them to the kids in the street. I would then open the tea caddie and refill his tobacco tin with tea leaves, no tea bags in them days, and give his tobacco tin a good shake.

One day Dad rolled and lit a cigarette, it smelt like a tea shop, like the smell you get when you walk into a café.

"Bloody hell," Dad said as he coughed, looking quizzically at his roll up. "What the hell has happened to my tobacco?"

He stood up and went for his tin in the pantry on the top shelf, and opened it, "Okay, who has put tea in here?"

We all sat and looked innocently at one another.

My sister Stella got the blame. Another time, I was making ice lollies in the freezer, I was selling these to kids in the street and we had a house full of them. We also had a gang of boys playing in the front room.

Dad was now working in a shoe factory and Mum was in a cardboard box factory. Me and my brother would arrive from school about four o'clock and Mum and Dad about five, so in that time it was party time.

We were playing pirates in our house, all slurping ice lollies and I swung on the huge chandeliers we had in the front room, my mum's pride and joy.

They broke from the ceiling with a crack and sparks flying everywhere. My mother was brought out of work and I was sent to my room, grounded for two months.

I must admit I was a real boy, a terror, nothing bad or nasty, but always thinking of mischief.

Brian York, a school friend, said one day, "I have an old motorbike at home if you want it Binksy. But you will have to push it home."

I was only eleven years of age, so me and Pete Harrison, pushed this motorbike on a red-hot day all the way to my house.

Now this was no small motorbike, it was a Douglas Dragonfly, a huge 1000cc monster.

Behind my house there were miles of fields, and me and a gang of my friends used to take turns roaring around all these fields, down some gravel pits and through ponds.

My dad asked, "Can I have a go son?" We all

looked at one another: "Sure you can Dad."
So, I gave my dad a quick idea of the gears and the clutch.
"I know, I know," said Dad.
He revved and revved this motorbike, this huge Douglas Dragonfly and suddenly released the clutch. We all knew where this was going so we ran back into my garden. Dad shot off like a bat out of hell and straight through the garden fence of a neighbour two doors up and right through their green house. Dad left it there and ran home.
I had to make an excuse that some kids from another neighbourhood had taken it without me knowing, but it was so funny and we laughed for ages after that.

My sister Stella was scared to death of moths and so one afternoon Barry and I collected as many from the shed as we could and our friend's sheds and outhouses.
We had thousands and that evening and night many moths came into our bedroom with the window open and the light on.
Soon we had jars full of them.
The next night Stella was out on a date and we knew she had to be home by eleven, so at ten forty-five me and Barry crept into her bedroom and pulled back the covers and carefully, without killing them, placed around a thousand moths in her bed.
We returned to our own beds and waited. Mum

and Dad were already asleep.

Smack on eleven the front door opened. "Bye," said Stella to whoever her boyfriend was, she shut the front door and slowly climbed the stairs. We hid behind our bedroom door which was slightly ajar, we heard the bedroom light come on and we could see the light reflecting on the landing, then after a while there was a click and the light went out.

We sat and waited, and then suddenly the most blood curdling scream you have ever heard echoed throughout upstairs.

We opened the door to see Stella, in her nightie, run down stairs followed by hundreds of moths, she was screaming and screaming. Me and Barry, in our underwear and vests, sat peeping through the door giggling.

Mum ran out first, then Dad in his underwear. They ran down stairs, me and Barry quickly got back into bed and pretended to be asleep when the door banged open.

"Why? That's what I want to know, why the bloody hell did you do this?" Dad said.

I sat up in bed and pretended to rub my eyes, "Do what Dad?"

"Your sister is hysterical downstairs. It was not funny Dennis. Now I want you to apologise to her and clean that bloody bed of moths. Do you hear?"

So, I did, although I don't think she ever forgave me.

I did all sorts to my sister, like hiding a massive old fashioned tape recorder under her bed, with one of the first space countdowns recorded on it.

As Stella climbed into bed I climbed out of mine. The plug for the tape recorder was in a socket just outside her door; there were also two big speakers attached to the tape recorder and I had hidden the cable under the carpet best I could.

When Stella's light clicked off I waited a couple of minutes then crept out of my room, I switched the socket on and ran back to bed.

Barry and I hid under the bed clothes, giggling, as the whole house shook as we all heard, '3-2-1-WE HAVE LIFT OFF.'

The sound was deafening as the rocket's engines fired up, it sounded like being in the middle of a runway with a Jumbo jet flying close over your head.

Over the top of that all we could hear was Stella screaming as once again she ran, this time into Mum and Dad's room. Needless to say, I was grounded again, and the tape recorder handed back to my Nanna whom I'd borrowed it from.

CHAPTER 6 – Being different

I was still being stood in a circle on Sunday afternoons, even in Rushden. I was being told off regular by my grandmother who would listen intently to the messages I gave.

I was really fed up with having to do this and told Dad, and this started an argument which Nanna and Mum won.

At this time, I was about twelve years of age, and every Friday night I would have to collect a box of groceries from the International Stores on the corner of Queen Street in Rushden.

I had to carry this box home which meant crossing over Fosse Green to Balmoral Avenue where we lived. On Fosse Green, would be about six or seven boys, all a bit older than me, who would wait.

"Your family's weird, they're all witches. Are you a witch, Binksy?" they would shout.

Then they would grab the box of groceries; bread, potatoes, sugar and eggs would be scattered everywhere, my clothes torn, gums and nose bleeding.

I would limp home, the police would be called, but nothing was ever done. They all lived near one another at the bottom of our street, and sometimes as I passed, some of the fathers would be standing at the gates to their gardens, talking.

As I passed they smirked; they thought it was a macho thing that their boys used to beat me up.

One day my dad said, "Dennis, come here lad." And he took me in the garden. There was my cousin David, he was a boxing champion in school.

"Enough of all this. David is going to show you how to protect yourself." That was that. For months, I was going to school with a cut lip or a black eye from sparring with David.

One Friday evening Mr Bland from across the road called at our house. Mum answered the front door where he said: "I have just seen something I have been waiting months to see, your Dennis is down on the green knocking ten tons out of those lads."

My mum went to get her coat. "Audrey, leave him, he will be okay. Make them think next time, won't it?" Dad said to Mum, smiling.

They had approached me again and the biggest of the six walked right up to me, about an inch from my face. "I told you not to come this way again, witch," he said.

I looked over his shoulder and I could see the other five lads looking around to see if anyone was watching. Mick, the big lad in my face, bent slightly to take the box of groceries off me again. I grabbed a tin of baked beans as his hands were full with the box, and I bought it down with all my might onto the bridge of his nose. He fell to the floor, blood everywhere.

He was rolling from left to right crying, I then took a tin of peas in the other hand and belted another lad, then they all made a grab for me.

I just remember swinging these cans of peas and baked beans, some ran away, others were on the ground crying. I picked up all the food and took the box home.

It never happened again.

I began now to make excuses not to do the circle thing on a Sunday and would not come home if I was out. I would be in a friend's house, or doing what kids do, like riding my bike down the gravel pits, and slowly the circles and the messages seemed to fade.

At fifteen years of age I joined the Army, what is now called Junior Leaders. My mother was heartbroken, "You're only fifteen our Dennis. Why? Why? That's what I want to know. You're too young."

But Dad was proud of my joining up although I was a thin, pale, sickly looking lad.

In the end my papers were signed and I remember it was my father's birthday, October 18th 1963, as I set off for Wellingborough railway station.

Uncle Les took me in his car, and I remember

seeing Dad on his bike going to work and we passed him in Queen Street. I opened the window and although we had said all our goodbyes I shouted "Ta ta Dad." Dad just smiled and waved his hand.

Me, aged 17, in the Army, Dortmund

Soon I had arrived at Bury St Edmunds. I stood outside the huge brick wall and although I could not see anything I could hear a man screaming at the top of his voice, "Left right, left right, left right." Along with the sound of hundreds of hobnail boots crunching into the ground. I walked in, about five foot seven inches tall, white as a sheet and thin as a lathe and God it was so hard.

We had to bull our rooms at five every morning for inspection, the bugle would play *Reveille,* and our uniforms had to be immaculate.

I met some great friends, and really took to it.

At seventeen and a half I joined the Royal Army Ordnance Corps as a driver.

I wanted to be an ammunition technician but never had the education for it, so I used to do night classes to gain my Army Certificate of Education to enable me to become one.

I remember I was in Germany on an exercise. We were in a huge forest and we had to go to an outfit nearby, which was the Royal Artillery, and collect a missile known as 'Honest John.'

It was huge and on a trailer. We would have to hook it up to a Bedford three-ton truck and follow a path through the forest; this was marked by white tape tied to trees.

We would make our way to the Ordnance camp where it would be tested, and then we would drive it back.

One day I was returning a missile to the Artillery camp when I suddenly noticed the white tape had disappeared, and I was in a cul-de-sac of trees. I had to unhook the trailer, leaving it behind, and having just enough room to reverse and get the truck out. I returned to the Ordnance camp where I had just come from to get help to pull the missile out.

I drove up and down the route which was shown by white tape, I could not find where this cul-de-sac was, in the end we had Artillery guys and Ordnance guys searching, to no avail. The Sergeant Major came to me as I returned, after about the fortieth time of going up and down this route, "Okay Binks. What have you done with it?"

I just stared at him. "I have done nothing sir."

He leaned forward, about an inch from my face, and as he shouted, spittle hit my face. "Well, where is it?" He yelled.

"It is in the forest. I had to take it off sir."

Given that we were near the East and West German border, as it was then at that time, soon there was RMPs or Royal Military Police who took me into a green caravan that had now been set up. I could hear the thud of the blades of helicopters whirl over head as it got dark, I was sat down.

The RMP Sergeant said, "Do you want a fag?" And offered me a cigarette. I took it and he offered me a light, "It's Dennis, isn't it?"

"Yes," I replied.

I was now feeling very worried, nervous and shaking.

"We have had some reports that you have dated quite a few German girls back at Wulfen." (This was our home base, where I was posted in Germany). "Well yeah, and so have most of the other guys."

"We're not interested in them. Do you owe anyone any money? Any large sums?"

"No," I said bewildered by the question.

"Has any girl or her friends done any favours for you?"

I sat there, thinking 'What is he talking about?'

"No," I replied.

"Okay," he said and leaning back smiling to himself he then said, "but you know Allison, don't you?" I was nineteen and like all nineteen-year-old single soldiers I knew plenty of girls.

"Yes. I know Allison. I gave her a reading once."

He looked at me and his chair cracked forward back on all four legs,

"A reading? What do you mean?"

I said without thinking, "I am a Psychic."

He just fell back in his seat again and laughed, "A bloody Psychic and you can't find this Honest John?"

I replied, "It doesn't work like that."

"Oh, we know that Binks, so cut the crap where is it? Who have you met today? I want names, details."

Just then the caravan door opened and the other RMP stood there beckoning the one in front of me. They whispered together and he said, "Okay Binks get out of here, we have found it."

I walked out of that caravan on auto pilot. I was

still stunned by the seriousness of the situation.

The missile was found in a cul-de-sac, which had heavy foliage overhead.

Me and my mates in the Unit always found this amusing, that I was a Psychic and lost a forty-foot Honest John Missile. I never lived it down.

CHAPTER 7 - Early love

I had a good friend in the Army, Jim Stuart. We were an advance party from Germany setting up a camp for the main force in a small place called Shorncliffe near Dover, Kent.

Whilst we were at Shorncliffe Jim said one day, "Hey! Den. I live near here, a place called Herne Bay, let's see if we can get some buckshee time off."

We did, and we headed for Herne Bay.

That night we went out on the town, and early in the evening we met two girls in a pub.

During the conversation, Jim said to them, "You know, Dennis thinks he's a bit of a Psychic girls."

The one I was sitting with replied, "Oh! I love that sort of stuff, give me a reading."

I said, "No! let's not do this." They all laughed and Jim said, "I knew it was all phooey!"

I took the bait. "Okay Jean." I took her hand.

As I was talking I was aware of a man coming close.

"I'm Jean's father," he said.

"Your dad's here," I said.

Jean looked at me, eyes wide open. "But Dad's dead."

"I know love, but he is here so what you term death never happened. None of us will die."

Jim called out, "Good guess."

I looked at Jim. "Shhh!"

Jim sat back, still grinning.

I asked her father to come closer, and I was then aware of a man about five feet seven inches tall with thinning dark hair. He wore a suit, and was slim with a bit of a hooked nose, he also had a brief case with him.

I relayed this to Jean who sat back and said, "That sounds just like my dad."

He put on his glasses that sat on the end of his nose, I explained this to Jean who confirmed this.

By now Jim and the girl he was with were leaning forward, listening intently and the pub was empty apart from us four.

I was then shown a car on the hard shoulder of a motorway, and a lorry ploughing into the back of it.

Again, I explained what I had seen. Jean gasped, turned to Jim and said, "Did you tell Dennis about my dad?"

"No! I didn't even know he was dead, I haven't been home for over a year Jean, you know that."

Once again, I was taken to the car and her dad was sitting in the driver's seat. He had passed to Spirit there.

I looked at Jean, "He died instantly."

"Yes," she whispered.

Her father said, *"There was a big court case and the driver said I was pulling out."* I relayed this information to Jean, who by now was beginning to sob. *"In court, they tried to say I was pulling out onto the motorway from the hard shoulder, but when examined in the hospital my car keys were embedded in my leg, stuck in from the impact."*

I looked up at Jean, her mouth was wide open and she was still crying. Jim, by now, was sitting with his eyes wide open. Her father then said, *"Tell Gladys I am okay, I love my girls and was at Jean's sixteenth birthday party at the Railway Hotel."* I told this to Jean.

"Oh! Dennis, Gladys is my mum and I did have my birthday party at the old Railway Hotel."

Her father then went on to say, *"Tell Jean that I know she is going to Blackpool in September, to see the lights."*

Jean smiled and could barely whisper "Thank you."

Suddenly, I was aware of the atmosphere in the Railway Hotel.

I looked up and everyone was sitting quietly open eyed. I sat back, "Okay, that's how it happens."

Jim coughed, sat back and said, "Okay Den, get another drink in, mate," trying to lighten the mood.

We moved to another public house and at the end

of the night Jean gave me her telephone number and said, "Telephone me when you're back in Germany Den. Okay?"

Being a typical squaddie, I lost the paper and soon we were back in Germany.

I got into the boxing team, as this meant more leave at home. By now I was quite sturdy and a strong runner. The training was very hard and we had to get up at four am to run miles. Then I was into the gym for some sparring and a work out. I was becoming quite a muscular guy and had quick reflexes.

I was asked if I wanted to have a go at my first real fight by my coach, Sergeant Mann, he said, "Come on Binks you will walk it, it's three rounds that's all."

So, I did. We had to go to an Army camp in Senelager where the fights were taking place. I sat in the changing room located next to the hall where the boxing matches were held.

Along with me were all the other boxers, shadow boxing and loosening up. I did the same, some skipping and facing a huge mirror did some self-sparring.

I had a knot in my stomach and felt sick when all too soon Sergeant Mann appeared, "Okay Binks you're on, let's go, remember all what I taught you, keep that chin in and use your jab."

The bell rang and I came out for the first round.

My opponent was taller than me, so I knew I had to get past his long arms and get inside.

He kept moving round to the right so I was aware that I would have to catch him with my right hand. His punches had no power in them and I was not perturbed by them.

Suddenly, he dropped his right hand and wallop, he staggered, his gum shield fell out and he stumbled against the ropes, the referee quickly grabbed me and sent me to a neutral corner.

I looked over his shoulder and saw the other boxer's corner men in the ring already. He was out cold.

I waited about a minute then he slowly sat up. 'Phew!' I thought, relieved that he was alright.

I didn't even have a bruise.

The fight was stopped and we were brought to the centre of the ring, my hand was held up as the winner. I was led back to the dressing rooms to the cheer of all the other boxers on my team.

I went on from tournament to tournament, not all knockouts, some on points, but I hadn't lost a fight.

I was finally in Bicester, Oxfordshire, where I was entering the corps of champions boxing tournament.

I didn't get past the first round, there was a white flash and that was it. Just smelling salts and a towel around my neck.

Jean and I were married and we had a son, Scott,

but Jean had a hard time with being an Army wife and after a while she never accompanied me anywhere.

I used to turn up on leave and Jean would make a cup of tea and ask, "Do you take sugar in your tea?"

We didn't even know one another.

We drifted apart and eventually we divorced. However, I did see Scott every time I was on leave or in the country.

CHAPTER 8 - Sergeant's Exam

I quickly went through the ranks from Lance Corporal to Corporal and then to Sergeant.

This was the hardest twelve weeks I have ever experienced, twelve weeks in the Brecon Beacons for the third tape on my arm.

I remember at the end of it I looked seventy years old. I had run further with a Bergen and a full complement of battle order kit than ever before. The Gurkhas were always the enemy and they were and still are hard, aggressive, fit, fighting men, but when talking to them they were the gentlest and friendliest guys you could ever meet.

I remember the last exercise was a navigation one across the Brecon Beacons.

It was to cover all day and through the following night, running and walking in full battle kit, stopping at check points to get yet another grid reference and off again.

One of the check points was at a place called Abercrave (remember this, as it comes back to me later). We didn't know how many check points there were or what the time was for the exercise, so we had to try and pace ourselves.

I ran through ice and snow, through rivers and over mountains. Stopping time and time again and each time who ever manned the check point had a glowing fire, some soup on and they would say, "Look you're the last man, give me your stone and let's call it a night. You will never make it now." (We were handed stones with numbers on at the beginning of the course and any time you felt like going home, you could hand this stone in.

This meant you did not have to explain why you wanted RTU/Return to Unit).

I would ignore this, grab the piece of paper from the person on the checkpoint, quickly running back into the dark night and away from the fire and words to discourage me.

I would set my bearings to my next checkpoint, grabbing a couple of rolls with cheese or ham as I ran past and off into the night again. Finally, I remember climbing down this steep slope to see a car park at the bottom filled with army lorries and other runners like me, sitting or sleeping.

I was exhausted and I limped to the final checkpoint where my final time was taken.

I was there all day waiting for other would-be Sergeants arriving. Finally, the RSM (Regimental Sergeant Major…or God) called us all together.

We fell into three ranks and he stood at the front and centre.

He screamed at us: "Never in all my time here in Brecon on this course have I see such miserable times. For this," he said, as he turned and pointed to the distance, "we are heading for the snowy peak in the distance and gentlemen we will run, any man who feels he could not handle this, please hand your stones into Staff Peters."

Everyone looked at one another. I was cold, soaked in sweat, past exhaustion and weak as a kitten, as my adrenaline had dropped as I had now switched off.

Many guys approached Staff Peters and handed in the stone.

I said to my mate Eddie Gilbert, "Give me a hand with my Bergen Eddie."

"Only if you will get mine on too, you nutter."

And we grinned, eyes sunk in, white as sheets.

I tried to fit the Bergen in the holes in my back, where it had dug in earlier, and with wobbly legs and a determined grimace on my face I lurched up and we staggered to where other men were now lining up to begin what would be a gruelling, painful experience.

The RSM appeared in full battle kit, "You must keep up with me otherwise it's home for you."

He screamed, "By the front, double march."

We began running and looking to my right I saw about twenty soldiers that were not joining us.

We ran around the corner out of sight of the car park when the RSM screamed again, "Okay lads well done."

Just then a dozen trucks arrived, "I just wanted to see who had the guts to do this, I just wanted to

see who was prepared to have a go. You're all sergeants!"
I nearly cried with relief.
On the trucks were the guys that had handed in their stones. They were gutted.
The RSM walked along the ranks shaking hands; he came to me and said, "Well done Sergeant Binks. You're a member of the most unique club in the world. You're a rifle platoon sergeant."
I felt a lump in my throat. I shook his hand and came to attention, "Thank you, sir."
Later that night, the fifteen of us out of forty-five that began, had a mad, well-earned party and the next day I headed back to my unit.
After this I saw a lot of action over the years and I remembered a fat sergeant when I was a private, who always led from the back. I never wanted to do that. 'Lead from the front always,' I was taught.

I was in the Sergeant's mess one day, at Bassingborne near Cambridge, the depot and training battalion for the Royal Anglian regiment, when I received a telephone call.
I was now married to a girl named Jane and had a three-year-old daughter, Natasha.
Jane said, "I can't stand this anymore. It's the Army or me."
I tried to reason, but it was no good, she was serious.
I had an interview with the Company Commander, and within six weeks I was on my

way home, a civilian.

We had a house in Northampton and I got a job in an engineering factory profile cutting, using a template and blow torches to cut out shapes in steel.

This was a heavy, dirty job, but paid well, and I got on great with the other guys.

Sgt Binks

Chapter 9 - All change at home

One day I came home and it was all quiet. I thought Jane and Natasha, who was three years of age, had gone shopping.

When the telephone rang, it was one of Jane's friends. She said, "When is Jane coming for Natasha? She has been here since eleven o'clock."

I walked up to Kate, who had Natasha, as it was only a five-minute walk.

As I collected Natasha, I asked, "Where has mummy gone?"

Natasha replied, "I don't know, but she said she would be back."

I opened the front door to our home and stood in the doorway, my mind racing. Immediately, I noticed that on the shoe rack in the hallway Jane's shoes were missing. I had a knot in my stomach and ran upstairs, all her things had gone.

On the bed lay an old set of Carmen rollers, her wardrobe open and empty.

I had a terrible time with Natasha. Josie, another friend of Janes, looked after Natasha while I worked. I tried everything to find Jane but to no avail.

I contacted old Army friends to see if they had seen her. I had exhausted the trail.

I knew that Jane and a man were seen at Northampton bus station, getting on a bus heading for London. I couldn't go running around London looking, but Natasha was heartbroken.

I was assigned a child counsellor to help and slowly I became accustomed to being a single dad.

My mates tried to fix me up with all sorts of girls, some would have bright purple, punk hair. One looked like a librarian, but I wasn't interested in any of them.

My mother 'phoned every weekend and said, "Come stay with me over the weekend, that way I know you have both had some good meals."

One weekend I arrived and Mum said, "Me and Ray (my step dad) will have Natasha. Stella and Barry are at the band club tonight, go and relax for an hour."

So, I did. I sat with Stella, her husband John and my brother Barry. There was a dance on and across the floor I spotted dancing a tall, leggy, blue eyed blonde, about my age.

I got up after a dance had finished and having seen she was with another woman, I walked over to her and said, "My name's Dennis, do you fancy a dance?" She smiled and I looked deep into her blue eyes. She was beautiful.

"Sure," she replied.

We danced all night.

Her name was Evelyn, she lived in Corby, and was a single mother. She explained she had two children: Hayley who was thirteen and a boy of ten, named Lee. We swapped details and telephone numbers and at the end of the night we separated.
When I got home to Mum's house I rang her and we made a date.

I went to Corby to visit her and took Natasha. Evelyn was all over her, "Oh! Isn't she cute? How on earth could her mother leave her?"
I shrugged and explained what had happened. Later, her front door burst open and there stood this blonde haired, blue eyed, cheeky, young lad.
"This is Lee," Evelyn said.
Lee sat in the chair in the front room and Natasha wandered in. Straight away Lee was showing Natasha old dolls and toys Hayley used to have at Natasha's age.
They got on great, then the front door opened again and a young girl about thirteen years of age walked in, she looked the spitting image of Evelyn.
"Dennis," Evelyn said, "this is my daughter, Hayley."
"Hi," said Hayley smiling and she quickly turned to Evelyn: "Mum, Judy asked if I can stay over. Can I? Please can I go? Can I? Please, please."
Without even a breath. Evelyn smiled, "Okay, but ring me tonight. Okay?"
Hayley danced and whooped as she ran upstairs.

"Well that's my lot," Evelyn said, laughing.

Hayley and Natasha became very close and after months of going backwards and forwards from Northampton to Corby, and Evelyn and her children going from Corby to Northampton, we finally moved from Northampton to Corby.

We stayed with Evelyn and her family.

I got on well with Lee, we were in the local Danesholme club father and son pool team. We did a lot of swimming and I also had a keep fit machine in my bedroom and Lee and I would work out on this. We spent hours playing chess and on his small computer playing games. Lee was a real cheeky Charlie, he was very loving but had a rare sense of humour. He reminded me of myself as a child.

One scorching hot day I was doing some gardening when suddenly I was soaked, I turned and there was Lee, in his swimming trunks, with a huge water pistol.

I grabbed the hose I had been using and as Lee ran back around the corner to get me again I blasted him with a torrent of water, he giggled and ducked away around the corner again. Next, I was soaked from the bedroom window, then from over next door and the fence. We all ended up soaked. Hayley, Evelyn and Natasha all running around the garden, screaming and laughing as they all got caught in the cross fire between Lee and me.

Hayley and Natasha grew closer and closer. Hayley

was at the big school and Lee was getting ready to go from junior to senior school.

Natasha was four years of age as she walked into the Danesholme infants school. I had a lump in my throat as she turned and waved, but she loved it and she settled in very well, but I still needed a job.

Lee, aged 11, and Natasha

I was told that Asda in Corby was looking for security officers, I still needed work so, I applied for the job.

I was interviewed and the lady interviewing me said, "Have you ever thought about being a store detective?"

"No."

"Come with me," she said and took me for a walk on the shop floor. She was talking to me, asking me hypothetical questions, she then said, "You have the eye for this, and a sixth sense, I am offering you the job Dennis." I accepted it.

I flew home and Ev, as she was known to me, hugged me, "Well done, Mr Hyde in the women's underwear department." We both laughed.

I loved the job and I just knew when someone was 'at it.' I would walk towards the doors as a huge torrent of people walked in all together on a Saturday morning and I would just 'know'.

I would look at someone and 'ping' game on, and right in front of my eyes they would do the dastardly deed.

One day I had to ask for help as I had nine shop lifters in the office. The police were flummoxed.

A year later and Hayley was fourteen, her father, Tony, had paid for Hayley to go to Switzerland with her school. She loved it and had a great time. As Lee grew older and nearer to his turn for the trip, he too was handed paper work about a ski trip with the school.

Lee had a different father to Hayley, and Lee didn't have the same bond as Hayley had with hers. In fact, Hayley's father used to feel so sorry for Lee whenever he used to pick Hayley up to go somewhere, he would also take Lee. This was obviously before I came on the scene. So, one day Lee came home with a folder, placed it in the drawer with all the other obsolete paperwork and never mentioned anything.

I peeked and there were the details of a skiing trip to Italy. I spoke to Evelyn, and one Saturday morning when Lee came down to breakfast I was talking to Hayley about her trip to Switzerland and skiing.

I could feel Lee's eyes burning into me. I casually said to Hayley, "You didn't throw those Salopettes away did you?" (Salopettes are skiing trousers).

Hayley said, "No, they're still in my wardrobe."

"Good. Because I know someone who may need them."

I never looked or gave Lee a thing, I just turned to him after a minute or two and said, "Well, do you think they would fit you?"

Lee sat with a lump of toast hanging out of his mouth, "Do what? Me?" Pointing to himself. "Skiing? You're kidding Dad, ain't you?"

I smiled and said, "No I'm not. I have paid the money for the trip, you're all booked up to go to Italy with the school."

He dived off his chair, missed his footing and fell to the floor giggling as we all did. Happy memories.

After a couple of years, I was informed that the town centre security was looking for security officers.

This was a tough job. You had to patrol streets, alley ways and car parks. It was a fair-sized town centre and you would be out in the open, up to tackle anything. Well that was me, one hundred percent.

I applied and got the job.

True to its word we had to tackle anything and everything. I loved it. I would wake up about five in the morning put a jogging suit on and run between five and ten miles, return about seven am, take a shower, put my uniform on and go to work.

It was nothing on a wet Monday morning to go crashing to the ground with a shoplifter clutching a bottle of whiskey from Littlewoods.

One day we had a call on our radios to head for Littlewoods, as a theft was taking place. I waited at the back of the store where the market is. Suddenly the doors opened and a small, skinny guy went past me like a missile. I was a fast runner and gave chase. I ran down Cardigan Place but by the time I was at the front of Littlewoods this guy was miles away.

I just stared, and a policeman came up next to me, smiling, "Not trying to catch him are you Dennis?"

"Yeah, why?"

"He's a county cross country runner. We know him, don't worry we will catch him."

All I could hear was the other security officers laughing down their radios.

We were informed that on this particular Saturday there was going to be a quiet demonstration from an organisation. Everything seemed in order and I was with another security officer, high up and looking down, when I noticed another group of people gathering.

Suddenly, they were unrolling banners and about two hundred people charged at one another. It was a riot.

I contacted our control room to get the police and as there was only two of us, and about two hundred of them we observed, taking notes.

One day a supervisor's job came around and I was asked if I would take on the job, which I did.

As security officers left due to being hurt, or getting a job with better hours, I would ask the security manager if he would replace these guys with ex-forces men, which he did.

There was six of us: me an ex-Royal Anglian, two ex-Paras, an ex-Marine, an ex-Medic, and an ex-Guardsman. Their kit was immaculate, boots polished, uniform pressed, all carried note books, and all were aware of correct radio procedure, so out on the town we went.

We were soon receiving accolade after accolade from the shop keepers. We had tackled all sorts, from a drunk guy wielding an axe, to shop lifters trying to stab us with syringes full of blood.

I was called into the office and the manager explained that he had decided to join his brother in Bristol and that later that day the security company's director would be visiting and wanted to talk to me.

He called me into his office and I was asked if I would consider the job of security manager. I did.

Many of my guys had been hurt in what had seemed like a trivial incident turning into a gang. During these incidents, we really were fighting for our lives. I recall one such time we had caught three shop lifters, all guys, and had to get them off the street. We had one by an arm each, me and a guy called Ted, an ex-Marine.

As we were walking him back, the shop lifter head butted Ted on his left cheek bone, causing what is known as a ping pong ball fracture, you know when you push in the top of a ping pong ball a small piece caves in? This is what happened to Ted's cheek bone and he needed a massive operation to repair this.

I spoke to the director and said, "If I consider this post then my security officers should carry handcuffs, and be taught self-defence."

He sat for a moment and said, "Leave it to me. Okay?"

I did take over as security manager and I met with the Corby Police and Inspector Thoroughgood. I explained to him the problems that we were experiencing, that there were times when me and my security officers would be struggling to retain someone whilst waiting for the police to arrive.

Although I understand how busy the police are, if this person has committed a serious offence on the town centre then the owners would expect us to arrest, control and restrain them.

Mr Thoroughgood stated that he had no problems with town centre security officers carrying hand cuffs if we had some training.

A self-defence instructor's course was organised at the police headquarters in Wootton, Northampton. And guess who got selected to do this? Yes, yours truly.

The course lasted for three weeks and it was gruelling. We had to run around a field a few times and then do warm up exercises, then we were taught how to bring a man to the ground and how to teach basic techniques.

At the end of this course I was eager to teach my security officers new ways of defending themselves. So, every Saturday morning between seven-thirty and nine I taught self-defence. I thought nothing of getting up at four in the morning, filling a Bergen up with about forty pounds of sand bags then running around the ring road of Corby which was about seven miles.

On route, there was a foot path that led to a wooded area. Here I would do fifty to one hundred press ups and carry the same log each time across my shoulders, do fifty dips, then continue around the ring road and end up sparring with a punch bag in the spare room. I would then shower, get dressed in my uniform and off to work.

One Saturday morning there was a tall man standing there in a jogging suit. He introduced himself, "Hello Dennis, I'm Andy Poole. I'm the self-defence instructor for Northamptonshire Police. I have been asked to see how you guys are getting on."

"Ask them yourself," I replied.

Andy took the security officers on self-defence training while I caught up with some paperwork.

At the end, he came into the office covered in sweat, he sat down and said, "You've done a great job Dennis, they're really good, well done. Have you enquired about the use of hand cuffs?"

"Yes."

Andy handed me a small catalogue which had information on various types of handcuffs we could use and by the following week all the guys were carrying hand cuffs.

The first time we used them was in 'Littlewoods.' We were called to someone making threats to a member of staff.

On arrival, I could hear the racket this man was making from outside the store. I entered and I walked into the area sectioned off by glass and wine bottles known as the 'Wine Shop.'

Two of my security officers were already there trying to talk to the man who was about six foot three inches tall, and powerfully built. As soon as I walked into the wine shop the man turned to see who had come in. He walked towards me, shouting, "You've ran all this way just to get a good kicking."

My two security officers went straight into action

as I had trained them, two at the back and me at the front. They both grabbed an arm and forced them straight into the air behind the man making him bend forward.

I grabbed his head so when he fell to the floor he wouldn't hurt himself. As soon as he was down, they brought an arm each up his back and clunk-click every trip, he was restrained in hand cuffs.

You could see the fight go out of him as soon as he knew they were on. We sent for the police and explained what had happened. A statement was taken from the lady working behind the counter. The police placed their own hand cuffs on the chap and we removed ours. At no time was the person free to harm anyone. It had to be a serious case for handcuffs to be drawn, but they were used on many occasions.

I remember being called to Spencer Court in Corby. The newsagents had just had a shoplifter in, a well-known shop lifter that could be nasty.

Myself and Ian arrived there at the same time and sure enough the thief was outside still arguing with the shop keeper and he had a bag full of jigsaw puzzles, toys and chocolate.

I approached him and said, "Come on mate, let's go back in the shop quietly."

He suddenly turned and his jacket opened. I thought he had a Stanley knife in his belt but when he pulled it out, it was a silver axe with a rubber covered handle.

He took a swipe, missing my chest by a hair's

breadth. Ian kicked the back of his knee and he stumbled, I grabbed the axe and Ian grabbed the shop lifter. We all fell to the floor, and on went the hand cuffs.

I was called to Littlewoods one morning at about nine-fifteen. On the radio, I was informed a woman had stolen a bottle of Johnnie Walker whiskey. When I was just around the corner from Littlewoods, a woman ran past me with a bottle of whiskey in her hand.

She was gone like a shot and I could see her taking swigs as she was running. I caught up with her in a matter of seconds and she had drunk the lot. She sat down, completely drunk and began singing, "Who's sorry now?"

When the police arrived, they could not help laughing as she was such a character.

I was given the news at home about now that Evelyn was pregnant.

Evelyn had a bad time carrying the baby and around the five month mark she began to get pains and her doctor booked her into the maternity unit at Kettering general hospital.

Ev had a job getting her shoes on and had to wear flip flops. I remember pulling up at the maternity unit in the hospital and it was thick with fog, a real pea souper. I grabbed Ev's bag and, taking her arm, we slowly walked into the maternity unit. The nurse said that Evelyn required bed rest and gave

her some pethidine. After a while Evelyn became woozy and sleepy, so I kissed her, grabbed my coat and left the maternity unit. The fog was now so thick you could hardly see car head lights. I was walking across the car park and got to my car, I was searching for my car key on the bunch in my hand when I heard a distinctive sound, it was flip-flop, flip-flop, and in the thick fog I just managed to see Ev, with her head on her chest wobbling towards me. As she got to me she rested her head on my shoulder and slurred, "I want to go home."
I said, "You can't sweet heart, come on, back to your bed."
And slowly we walked back to the maternity unit.
I explained to the nurse, who said, "Naughty girl, she must have slipped out when no one was looking."
Ev was tucked back into bed, I kissed her again and she went off into a slumber. Off I went again and as I reached my car, in the worst fog I have ever experienced, I could her flip-flop, flip-flop and once again, looking like a zombie in the films, Ev was by my side.
Three times this happened until in the end the nurses said she was allergic to pethidine.
Soon after this she settled down and four months later the baby of the family was born: Craig, on June sixteenth. My birthday was June thirteenth and Lee's June twenty first, Summer Solstice day.
At about this time Lee was beginning to behave strangely, he became difficult to talk to and

argumentative. We put it down to teenage blues as he was about fifteen now.

CHAPTER 10 – Unified Fighting Systems

One day I was walking through Everest Lane car park, on duty, when I saw a group of guys walking between the cars placing flyers on the window screens. We had told not to allow this as when it took place many people removed flyers and threw them to the ground, and cleaning was a problem afterwards.

I approached this little man who seemed in charge, I say little as he was about five foot eight inches tall but slim and wearing glasses.

I said, "Excuse me, do you have permission to place flyers on cars in the town centre?

"No," he replied, "I didn't think I had to have permission."

I replied, "Well you do, now can you please remove these?" Gesturing with my hand around the car park. "Certainly, not a problem." And so they did.

There was one on the floor and I picked it up and read it. 'Unified Fighting Systems, taught by Andy Gibney.' On it was a picture of the guy I had just spoken to.

I stared at it. I could do with some new ideas, and

to brush up on my self-defence, I thought and I also read that they held classes at the Danesholme Centre.

I lived on the Danesholme estate and knew where the centre was, so on the following Monday night I turned up with jogging bottoms, a sweatshirt and a towel in a bag.

I met Andy and he laughed, remembering me approaching him in the car park. There were about thirty people, all ages, all sizes, men, women and children.

So began my training with UFS. I was getting on great, I would get up at five in the morning put on a pair of shorts, a vest and trainers, do some warm up exercises, and then run up to eight to ten miles. I would return, do two hundred press ups and two hundred sit ups, take a shower and go to work. On Monday, Wednesday and Saturday I would train with UFS.

I was getting well into this and I had begun taking an interest in stick fighting and I had won a number of tournaments.

One day Andy said, "I want to enter you for two British titles, they are both stick fighting contests." I was over the moon, I was by now forty-five years of age, but fit as a fiddle and looked about thirty.

I trained even harder, running at night when I was not training and doing more stick fighting.

The day arrived. I got on board a coach in Kettering town centre and we set off for the Vauxhall Leisure Centre in Luton. I won the first two fights but I was beaten in the semi-final for the British championship by a guy named Sparrow, who I later learned was the British champion.

Part of the team. I'm in the middle

At the end of the event – with medals

Everything was going great and at night I was working on night club doors as a bouncer.

I knew a guy from Northampton named Arthur White who used to take on bouncers to work in night clubs. I would wear a black suit, a dickey bow and white shirt. I would work alternatively at Opus Two and Cinderella Rockefeller, both very busy night spots and again my self-defence training came in handy.

People do the most stupid things when they are drunk, although I was never one of those bouncers you used to hear about years ago, who used to beat people up just for the fun of it. However, if they took a swing at me I would very quickly restrain them and send them on their way unless the police were called and usually there was a police van parked outside.

One night a guy came up the steps of Rockerfellers, and walked straight up to me. He said, "You're the b****** that beat my mate up last week."

I tried to explain that I was not even working that night, but he was growing angrier by the minute. I was joined by Ted, a huge guy, who looked very intimidating, but that didn't even phase him. Suddenly he grabbed me by the collar of my jacket; I gave him such a strong upper cut he took off and went down four steps. He slowly got up and staggered around, looking dazed. I went down to see if he was okay, he looked concussed.

I said, "Look mate, get a taxi and get home.

Okay?"

Suddenly he swung around and brought a knife out of his jacket. I backed away quickly and in a second there were five of us. He looked around and as he slowly backed away he mumbled, "I'll get ya."

And that was that, or so I thought. In the day time, I managed my security officers, catching shop lifters.

One day we had a call on the radio to go to Foster Brothers, a men's wear shop.

I arrived first and the manager was standing at the door, he just shouted, "He's gone that way Dennis," pointing up the street.

"What did he look like? What was he wearing?" I asked.

As the manager was relaying the details I was also passing it over the radio to my other security officers. I ran to the top of the shopping mall and I saw the back of a man, answering the description given to me, disappearing around the Civic Centre heading towards the woods.

I was joined by Tony, another security officer and we both ran to the woods. We stood still and I heard a noise behind a wall next to an advice centre. I quietly crept around the wall, and low and behold there was the same guy I had had the fracas with at the night club, the one with the knife.

He looked at me quizzically and just said, "You?" He made a run for me; on the ground were about five men's jackets. As he came near I just moved back a bit, he took a swing, I side stepped and brought a right cross on his chin. There was a sickening crunch, he staggered back and from the jackets on the floor he lifted a bottle of vodka, a full one.

He brought it back to take a swing, when the lady store detective from Littlewoods came from behind and grabbed the bottle. By then I was aware of my other security officers; we grabbed him, restrained him, and placed handcuffs on him.

The police arrived and I related what had happened and he was taken away.

It was about now I was suffering with my right shoulder. I would have a terrible job putting on my shirt or coat. It then spread down the small of my back as well.

I was having difficulty even sitting down and I was spending more and more time now in the office and less on the town centre.

I went to see my doctor who examined me and said, "It looks like arthritis, Mr Binks."

"Arthritis?" I said, frowning, "How do I get rid of it?"

And then the damning words of the doctor: "You don't. You live with it. I can send you for x-rays and take it from there as to the medication."

That is what happened, but slowly it grew worse. I couldn't lay properly or sleep. I was up all night and going downstairs was a nightmare.

I would spend half of the night sitting up and watching television. One day I was in the security office when through the window, I observed the operations manager and the personnel manager heading to my office.

I was asked into another room and as soon as I saw the brown folder containing my medical files, I knew. Mick Jones, the operations manager, explained, "Dennis, we know how you love your job, and you're renowned all throughout the company, but I am afraid, due to your ill health, we have to let you go. Our insurance company will no longer cover you."

I was heartbroken. Once I used to run across the Brecon Beacons with seventy pounds on my back, full kit and a rifle, now I had a job placing one foot in front of the other.

CHAPTER 11 - Lee

Lee was about eighteen now and living with his girlfriend, Claire. They looked so right for one another and had a beautiful home.

Lee was working as a plasterer. Craig was seven years of age, it was Christmas 1995 and Lee telephoned us on Christmas Eve and said he would be up to see us over Christmas on Christmas Day or Boxing Day.

He never showed up for either.

As usual, on Boxing Day we would go to the Danesholme club. We had been there about ten minutes when the doorman came to our table, he said, "Dennis, there is a man at the door asking for you, he said it's urgent." I looked at Ev and limped out. Standing just inside the door was Glenn, Claire's father.

He said, "Oh Dennis I don't know how to tell you, Lee is at Kettering general hospital he has taken an overdose and is in a coma."

I said, "Drugs?" Glenn just nodded. I hobbled back into the room where my family was and in minutes we were flying in cars heading towards Kettering.

Evelyn and myself first went to see Lee. I have never seen so many pipes in someone's mouth.

"He has to go to the John Radcliffe hospital in Oxford. We cannot deal with this here, he may have a bleed in his brain and he has pneumonia," said a doctor.

Lee was rushed to Oxford and we followed in cars.

"Drugs?" Ev said, "what the hell are they on about? Drugs? Lee doesn't do drugs."

I thought about the mood changes and how argumentative Lee had become, like sitting on a time bomb sometimes. We put that down to teenage blues, but it wasn't.

Lee was in Oxford for three weeks and was then transferred to the Swindon hospital as they had sedated Lee to allow his brain to heal.

Lee had a swollen brain and pneumonia. He was at Swindon for a week when we received a telephone call, "We are reducing the sedatives tomorrow, we need someone here when he wakes up."

Ev said she could not do it on her own as we had been told that no one knew if any brain damage had occurred. We all went to Swindon.

Evelyn, Natasha, who was now twelve years of age, Hayley, who was twenty-four and Claire all waited in a side room, while I sat by Lee's bed from about 11am until 3pm when he began to stir.

Slowly he looked up, he could only open his left eye.

" Dad," he said, looking around.

I leaned forward, took his hand, "Hiya Lee, you're okay son."

Lee looked around again and then peeped under the bed sheets, he began to cry, really sobbing. "What's the matter?" I said.

Lee looked up with only his left eye open, "I've got no clothes on Dad." He was really heart-broken; I pushed back a screen and yelled, "Can I have some clothes please for my boy?"

A pair of pyjamas were brought and he was soon sitting up, talking sips of water.

I quickly went and fetched all the girls sitting outside waiting.

"He's awake okay? But he can only open one eye at the moment."

Ev sobbed: "Why?"

Before I could answer the nurse came out and asked us back in.

Lee was sitting up now and couldn't remember anything.

A doctor came around and explained that Lee was very lucky, he certainly could have died. He also told us that his other eye would soon open, and it did.

Lee came back to our local hospital and was soon discharged, but there was a distinct change in him; the Lee that came back was not the Lee that went, and now we had the drugs to worry about.

We were called to Lee's home one night and Claire said he had trashed the house and leapt out the window. Apparently, Claire would not give him any money for drugs.

He was found later that night in the toilet in McDonald's, taking just one breath a minute.

He was in hospital for a couple of days and I went with his mother to collect him. He looked white and thin: "Come on home with us Lee. Spend as much time as you want with us. Okay?"

Lee smiled and said, "Okay Dad."

It was like old times, Lee, Craig and Natasha all giggling and playing music in their bedrooms.

Hayley now had her own place. Her father, John, had provided for her and Hayley now worked for him as he had his own company.

Hayley was getting ready to get married to Jack. He seemed a great guy and we all had to go to Wellingborough, where Haley lived, for the wedding rehearsal at the church.

During the rehearsal, the minister asked about the four hymns or songs Hayley had selected.

Hayley looked puzzled and said, "We have only chosen three."

The minister said, "Take home the hymn book and select your fourth hymn or a suitable song you would like and return the hymn book and your selection to the rectory on Monday." The rehearsal being over, we left the church.

I said to Hayley, "Have you any ideas on what hymn you want?"

Lee, walking behind, said, "*Imagine* by John Lennon."

We all stopped and looked at him. "Why that

one?" I asked.

Lee just smiled and said, "I would like it at my funeral."

We all laughed and called him a silly idiot.

Lee was still at our home but it wasn't long before he wanted to go home to Claire. We could all see a definite change in him; people had to tip toe around him and he was very explosive.

Photos of Lee

Lee returned to his home with Claire. They both loved one another very much, but all too soon another phone call came then another and another.

In 1999 Lee was admitted onto the Addington Ward at Kettering hospital nineteen times.

Ev and I made an appointment to see a head doctor, Dr Scanlon. We pleaded with him to section Lee.

All he spoke of was death and dying young, he had hung from the top of the multi-story car park by his fingertips, twice.

Once Claire, on bended knees, had pleaded with him to get him back, but the next time that wasn't enough. It took two police officers to talk him back.

He had also jumped in front of a double decker bus in Corby and when it stopped and did not run over him, he jumped on board the bus and beat the driver up.

Here we were now, pleading with the authorities to lock our son up as we knew this was the only way to save his life.

Dr Scanlon looked up from Lee's notes, some from a psychiatrist that had been handling Lee and some from Lee's own doctor. "I am sorry but due to the Mental Health Act of 1983, if drugs are being used, is this a mental health reaction? Or is he doing this through drugs? If it is through drugs, then we cannot section Lee."

Ev and me sat there from 2pm until 6.30pm pleading, but on no account would Dr Scanlon budge.

"You know you're sending Lee to his death?" I said.

"Maybe," replied Dr Scanlon, "but until we get hard proof that it is a mental problem not a drug problem then we cannot handle it any other way."

We left knowing Lee was in Addington ward. We went home dejected, feeling guilty for trying to section Lee but at the same time knowing that he was a danger to himself.

CHAPTER 12 - New Year's Day

Schizophrenia started to take place with Lee. Claire said he would wake up in the night and, whilst she slept, he would go down stairs.

Claire would wake up and hear someone talking. She said, "I would go down stairs and there was Lee, in the pitch dark, talking to an empty chair."

Also, he would be found sitting stark naked in the middle of the night looking at the moon and talking to 'Ghosts' as he put it, in their garden.

He would say that Claire's mother and father were plotting to kill him and he would sit in his chair watching television with a knife up his sleeve in case they visited.

One day Lee had trashed their home again and was upstairs. Claire was terrified and called the police. Lee jumped from the upstairs window as the police entered the house and ran down the street. They caught him and Lee was taken to Kettering general hospital again.

This time he hit two orderlies, knocked out the two policemen with him and threw the trolley he had been laying on through a huge window of the hospital. He jumped through it and made his escape, until, once again, ended up in Addington ward. All this was passed onto Dr Scanlon and another meeting took place, an even longer one, but again even with all this going on they would not budge.

Lee would lay his head on my shoulder and sob, "I am so, so sorry Dad. I don't mean to hurt anyone."

I would stroke his head and say, "We know that Lee. We all love you. Remember this much, this is your home you can always come home no matter what you have done, we will not turn our backs on you. Look at me, do you understand?"

Lee wiped his face, "Yeah, of course I know that Dad."

He loved his mum so much, they were really close. Claire mentioned many times how much he spoke about his mother and how all this was hurting people.

We come to Christmas again; it was December 2000, and we had Lee and Claire with us on Boxing Day. It was like old times, playing tricks on one another, we had a board game called *Forfeits* and it was hilarious.

Lee and Claire left at about 11pm, he hadn't had a lot to drink and seemed in great humour.

On December 28th Claire telephoned and said Lee wanted to see us, so Evelyn and I went to their home. Lee had loads of clothes out and was saying, "Here you go Dad. I have never worn this."

Lee was always impeccably dressed, he always had

smart new clothes on.

I said, "Don't you want these?"

Lee shook his head, "Nah, got to have a clear out, got too many."

I took a couple of sweatshirts and we headed home. "Come and see us over New Year's Day." We told Lee as we were leaving.

New Year's Day came and Ev texted Lee on her mobile: 'Happy New Year Lee, how are you?"

His reply was, 'Fed up, no money, a lousy new year.'

Ev then replied, 'Come up to our house then, and have something to eat and see a video, you and Claire.'

We didn't get a reply.

I was on my computer in our bedroom just surfing, looking through web pages. It was about 9 or 10pm New Year's Day evening.

Suddenly I felt a real blow of cold air on the back of my neck. I looked around and as it was January 1st, it was freezing outside, but no windows or doors were open and the central heating was on.

I saw my own reflection in the dressing table mirror, smiled to myself and thought 'Stupid idiot.' I returned to the computer. About five minutes later I heard Evelyn give a blood curdling scream from downstairs, "Dennis!"

I flew to the door and downstairs, our telephone was in the hallway outside our living room. As I came down the stairs I could see Ev holding the telephone by the flex with the hand set dangling down, her eyes where full of tears.

I asked, "What's wrong?"

All she could do was whisper, hardly audible, "Lee's dead."

I flew into a rage, who was this? It must be a joke. I grabbed the hand set and screamed down the telephone, "Who is this?"

A voice I knew sobbed: "Oh God Dennis I am so, so sorry mate, but Lee is dead. It's Glenn here. He fell from the top of the multi-story car park."

"Where are you now?" I asked.

Glenn said, "We are just leaving the police station, Dennis, and going home."

"Okay, we will see you at your house."

I turned to Evelyn, who was shaking and sobbing and held her. She felt so fragile in my arms, like china that would break at any moment. Craig was upstairs on his computer, or Playstation, unaware of the tragedy that had just happened.

I called him down, put on his coat and explained to him we had to go out and he would have to stay with our next-door neighbour, Thelma.

We asked Thelma and she had no problems taking care of Craig, who was 12 years of age now.

We went to Glenn and Dee Dee's (Dee Dee is Claire's mum) home.

"What about Natasha?" I said to Ev and Hayley.

We knew that Natasha was in a night club with all her friends. I telephoned the night club, which was *Martine s* at the time, and asked if they could put on a screen or loud speaker for Natasha to contact us. In the meantime, myself and Evelyn set off in the car.

On the way, my mobile telephone began to ring. I pulled over, it was Natasha.

"What's wrong? Why did you have them call me?"

I replied, "Meet me outside *Martine s*. I will explain when I get there."

We pulled up outside *Martine s* and Natasha climbed into the car with a plastic horn and tinsel on her that you would get at a party; she seemed giggly and slightly drunk.

"I want you to prepare yourself for this," I said as we sat in the car with sounds of music and people singing and laughing around us. "Prepare myself for what?" Natasha said, not understanding the gravity of the information that was coming to her.

I coughed and prepared myself as well, "Lee died tonight."

Tash, as she is known, suddenly went rigid. "What did you say?" She asked as she was sitting in the back of the car.

She leaned forward, "Say that again."

"I said Lee died tonight Tash. He fell from the top of the multi-story car park."

Her face creased up and she just sat there with nothing happening, then it started. She was screaming, shouting, and punching the seats. "Okay, okay sweetheart. Look we are going to see Claire at Glenn's and Dee Dee's okay? So, we have to be brave." I cuddled her head on my shoulder

as sobs racked through her body, in amongst her crying she was sobbing, "Oh Lee. Lee why? Why?"
I said, "Come on sweetheart. We have a lot to do."
Tash sat back, "Okay Dad, I am okay Mum. Oh! Mum."
And Tash started crying again as she looked at her mother. The pain was unbelievable but I had to hold them together. I remembered times in the Army when through a campaign or theatre of war there had been deaths and casualties.
I was used to keeping order, best as it could be with troops, but this was different. These where my babies; you never expect this to happen.

We soon pulled up at Glenn's home and climbed the stairs to the top maisonette.
As I stood at their door I looked to the left and there, right opposite, was the multi-story car park.
Glenn came to the door looking like the rest of us, white as a sheet. As I stepped over the doorway I could already hear the wailing and sobbing from inside.
I walked in with Ev and Tash behind me, Claire was on the sofa, completely and utterly shattered.
I found it hard to remember anyone in such a state, she was angry, she was sobbing, she began screaming and rocking.
I looked at Dee Dee and said, "She may need a doctor you know?"
Dee Dee nodded, cuddling Claire to her.
Claire seemed to settle a bit, her face bright red,

her eyes swollen. She was trying to control the tears by gulping in between breathing, she had a blanket around her.

"What happened Claire?" We knew they had been out all day and that Ev had texted Lee. Claire said, "We had a great day, but unbeknown to me Lee had taken some heroin this morning. Anyway, we went out, we were in the Phoenix pub, Lee was on tables singing and dancing, he was in a great mood. He met all his mates and it was a great day. We then went to see my nan."

Claire had to stop as she was overcome again, sobbing and talking incoherently.

We waited. She went on: "Lee fell asleep at Nan's and I had to wake him up. He seemed a little narky, he was in a mood."

Claire than took a sip of water from her dad, who as he passed me, rubbed my shoulder.

She then continued, "We took a short cut through the woods to get back here as I had left the keys to our home here. Suddenly Lee began arguing, about rubbish, next thing he punched me so hard I fell to the floor, and then for the first time ever in his life he kicked me. I was so winded I couldn't breathe."

Claire began to sob, and then regained herself again, "Lee lifted me up but I was so winded I was like a rag doll in his arms, he kept saying 'I am so sorry Claire, I don't know what I was doing.' I was scared. I had just been punched and kicked and I knew Lee could go off again at any moment, so I broke free and ran towards the lights, to McDonald's and *Martine's* night club." Claire again had her face in a towel sobbing.

I held Ev in my arms as this horrific story unfolded. Claire was Lee's rock, how she stood by him for five years throughout all this I will never know.

Claire looked up and carried on, "Lee caught up with me outside McDonald's and grabbed my handbag, he kept saying 'give me the keys.'

I explained to him the keys were at Mum and Dad's.

Claire looked down wistfully and whispered, as if talking to herself, "If only I had the keys, he could have gone home."

Her face turned to horror. "Claire!" called her mum, snapping Claire back, "You did everything you could baby." And cuddled her.

Claire continued, "Lee's face suddenly went blank, like no feeling, like a robot. He said, 'I am going to end this, I have hurt so many people, please forgive me and always remember I will always love you.'"

Claire began sobbing again, recalling this was so painful. She looked up and Dee Dee said, "Are you okay? Do you want to go on?" Claire nodded. "At that Lee turned and walked away. He turned once and stood for a minute looking at me and he was gone. I was so scared I was frightened of following him. I had just been beaten up."

Her voice was going up and down as she was

talking and crying at the same time and then she began sobbing again, uncontrollably rocking backwards and forwards.

With her face in a towel she regained herself, trying to stifle the sobs.

"I telephoned my dad, and told him what had happened, and Dad said walk to the police station and I will meet you, which I did. We walked down Elizabeth Street right opposite the multi-story car park and I heard Lee call out 'Claire' twice. I froze, looking up at the multi-story but it was pitch black and the echo seemed to come from everywhere."

Claire sat up a bit, then, regaining her composure, she wanted to tell me and his mother everything. "Dad said 'Let's get you home and I will go and look for him.' Well Dad got home here and called Steve." (Steve was a lodger staying at Glenn's and Dee Dee's and we all knew him).

Glenn continued the story; he was leaning over the back of the sofa that me and Evelyn was sitting on. We turned to look at him as he continued, "I said to Steve that 'Lee is being a plonker again, give me a hand to get him home.'

So, Steve put his coat on and off we went, I thought we can take a short cut through the bus station, so that is where we both headed. Laying on the ground beneath the highest point of the car park I saw Lee lying on his back. As me and Steve walked up I could see blood from his nose. I thought he had been in a fight and been knocked out.

I was about to kneel down to him when suddenly there were dozens of police men running up to me and Steve.

'Don't touch him.' A policeman called as he ran up to us, then out of nowhere an ambulance arrived.

What the hell was going on? I thought.

The policeman knelt beside Lee and felt the pulse in his neck and said, in the mic piece of his radio, the words that made me freeze. 'We have a fatality here Sarge.'"

Glenn began to sniff and wiped away the tears from his eyes, you could see the pain in his face.

He went on, "I knelt down by him and said 'why boy why?'

Then they placed a tent around him and photographs were taken. A hearse arrived and Lee was taken away."

We all sat there shocked, Ev was just sitting staring at the wall, the silence so loud.

A knock came to the door, Glenn answered and we could hear him talking, a policeman entered.

He took a pocket book out, he coughed, you could see he found this difficult.

He said, "This is never easy, I don't know what to say to any of you, but I do have to say that a man was found at the bottom of the multi-story car park in Anne Street at about nine twenty this evening, and that man has been identified as Lee David Jack."

CHAPTER 13 – Bump in the night

We arrived home at about two thirty in the morning; Natasha went straight to bed. I had to telephone Hayley and break this tragic news to her.

I dialled her number and it rang and rang, then the sleepy voice of Hayley.

"Hello, who is this?" she said, a little annoyed at the time.

"Hayley, it's Den."

Hayley went quiet for a minute.

I prepared myself, "Are you sitting down?" I said.

"Why what's up?" She said, her voice jerking into life.

"Look it's Lee, Hayley. Lee died tonight, about nine fifteen."

There was quiet and I could hear her crying like a child, hardly audible. "How?" she asked in sobs.

I explained in detail everything that had taken place. "We will be over tomorrow okay Hayley?"

I felt so hopeless, she lived about forty-five minutes' drive away, and I wanted to stay with Ev

that night as she had gone so quiet.
I said to Hayley, "Look I don't want you there on your own, call your friend Michelle to stay with you." Haley replied, "No, I will be okay."
I was firm with her thought and said, "Please for us, so we know someone's with you sweetheart okay?" She agreed.
Craig was staying the night next door and me and Ev stood in the kitchen. I made a coffee and said, "We have rehearsed this, haven't we? We knew this day would come."
Ev looked down, "Oh yes I knew he wanted to die, but no one else seemed to care," (meaning the authorities). I held Ev and we went to bed. As I opened the bedroom door I noticed the computer was still on and suddenly I recalled earlier that evening sitting there and experiencing someone blowing on my neck.
No, I thought, it couldn't be.
I switched it off and tried to sleep. I slept fitfully waking up with a start, Ev was also sleeping and waking.
The next day I had to telephone the rest of our family and go over to see Hayley.
We went to Hayley's first. Hayley has four boys; all great guys. Anthony at the time was eight years of age, Brandon six, Jack three and Daniel one.
Hayley met us at the door and fell into her mother's arms. Natasha, Hayley and Ev all sat on the settee holding one another sobbing.
"Den, are you okay?" Hayley said. "Yeah, I'm

fine," I replied. But my concern was Evelyn, she was too calm, too quiet. We explained everything to Hayley. She took it in, but didn't seem shocked, she too had taken it too well.

It was getting late, I said, "Have you got anyone to stay with you?"

She explained her friend Michelle had popped out so we could be alone, but was staying the week.

We gave her a hug and left for the car and she waved goodbye to us. I said, "That's enough for one day, let's go home."

As soon as we got in the house Evelyn began screaming, she was hysterical. Nothing I could say or do made any difference, she was in so much pain and hurt.

I called our doctor who came out immediately. He examined Ev and prescribed some Valium to get her through the next couple of days.

Ev's sister, Jackie, was at our door then. Jackie was the only relative Evelyn had, apart from the children. Both their mother and father had passed.

By now I had collected the medication from the chemist and in-between hysterics Evelyn took a tablet and within thirty minutes she was sleeping on the sofa.

Jackie looked at me and said, "You have got one hell of a job on your hands mister, with all these to take care of."

I nodded, but not expecting what was to come.

After about three hours Evelyn stirred, "Is my Lee

in the kitchen?" she asked.

Slury with the medication, her eyes hardly open and swollen with tiredness and crying, "Tell Lee I want him, I can hear him and Claire talking in the kitchen."

I did not have to say anything, you could see realisation sink in, even in her drugged state with taking Valium. She slowly turned her face into the cushion and began to quietly sob and slowly drifted off to sleep. This went on for days. Until one morning I woke up and Ev was drawing back the curtains.

Although the pain was etched on her face, she said, "I have got other children here and their needs don't go away."

And the slow road to recovery began. It was pitted with many falls but the healing had started.

Around the third day after Lee had died I received a telephone call from the undertakers in Shire Lodge, Corby. The Co-op undertakers. They needed to call and take details of Lee's funeral, so we arranged to see them that afternoon and no sooner had I hung up the telephone that morning the door knocked.

I answered it and it was the police officer who had called in to talk to us the night of Lee's death. He asked if he could come in as he required some details.

I looked at Ev and she nodded. The police officer came in, took out a note book and some paper work.

I asked him if he would like a cup of tea, and he agreed. I soon made three cups of tea, and we sat wondering why he had called. He said, "On the night Lee died, how did he seem? Did he contact you?"

Ev said, "I texted him on my mobile, I asked him if he was okay, and he answered he was depressed."

The police man said, "He telephoned for an ambulance before he fell, did you know?"

Me and Ev looked at one another, "He rang an ambulance?" I said.

The police man turned over the pages of his note book and said, "Yes, from the telephone outside *The Corinthian* public house."

I knew where that was and so did Ev. "Why?" I asked.

"Well, the emergency operator took a 999 call at around 9.09 that night and a man saying he was Lee Jack said that he was going to jump from the top of the multi-story car park in Corby, and for them to send an ambulance as the car park is deserted on normal days and it will be even more deserted on New Year's Day eve. He said he wanted an ambulance because if he should survive the fall he did not want to lay in agony for hours until someone found him."

A shiver went up my back and I felt Ev next to me begin to sob.

"There will have to be a post mortem," the policeman said, "also a Coroners enquiry."

I showed the policeman out the house. Ev was in a state again, she was taking these Valium and was wasted most of the day. I had no time to grieve with the family to hold together.

The following day there was another knock on the door, and a gentleman from the Co-op Undertakers was there. I had to sit and fill out a form for Lee's funeral.

"What colour material inside the coffin Mr Binks?" asked the undertaker.

"Err, a nice gold or cream colour," I said.

"And would you like a mention in the local paper?"

Ev had just been sitting there, drifting in and out, not really concentrating on anything really.

We looked at one another, "Sweetheart, what would you like to put in the paper?"

Her face just creased up and deep from within came slowly the most painful cry I have ever heard.

I turned to the undertaker and wrote 'Tragically, on 1st January 2001 Lee David Jack tragically died. All flowers to the Co-op Undertakers, Shire Road, Corby, Northants.'

The funeral man then said, "Where would you like the service?"

I looked at Ev, as Ev was a Roman Catholic.

She said, "Lee had never taken Holy Communion you know."

The funeral director sat for a minute, and I remembered Ev had told me where she went to school in Corby. In Occupation Road there was a church there called Our Lady of Walsingham Roman Catholic Church.

I asked Ev about this and she just nodded.

I said to the funeral man, "Can I call you later about this?" He nodded, handed me a copy of the form that was just filled in and said, "You can visit Lee tomorrow if you like at our Chapel of Rest in the Darley Dale."

I smiled and said thank you, shook his hand and walked with him to the front door.

I returned to Ev, she sobbed and said, "Why? Why?"

I held her and looked up gulping back the tears.

Natasha and Craig where also wandering around in a daze.

I sat them down and said, "We are all going to get through this together."

Craig was only twelve years of age. Natasha was nineteen.

They both looked at me with pain in their eyes, "You know we have to be brave for Mum, okay? But it's okay to cry, and to talk about this. Any time you want to talk, I am here. Okay?" They nodded.

The day came for us to visit the Chapel of Rest. I collected Claire, and the rest of my family. I was okay until I got there, and then I just couldn't look. I was so hurt, it would be too painful.

Ev said, "Okay sweetheart, don't worry." And together with Claire and Natasha the three of them stepped through the door.

I waited and after about ten minutes Ev came back

out, smiling.
I looked at Ev, she seemed better. She said, "He looks fine Dennis, are you sure?"
I gulped and said "Okay."
Ev came with me, Claire and Natasha where standing beside the coffin.
Lee was wearing his new black suit, brand new black shoes he had for Christmas, and he looked just as if he was asleep.
I broke down, "Why? Oh, Why man? Look at you. What have you done?"
As Ev brought me out I was aware of the heady sweet smell in the Chapel of Rest.

We came home, and my best mate Pete who had been up to see Lee with Jackie, Ev's sister, came around. "Come on Den, let's have a pint mate. Jackie will stay with Ev."
I looked at Ev, she smiled and said, "Go on it will do you good."
I went upstairs to get dressed and as I walked into our bedroom, I could smell that sweet heady smell again from the Chapel of Rest. I looked around quickly and it was gone.
Many times, after that, I would catch this smell around me.
One night I was fast asleep, when suddenly I was woken by the sound of loud music. I sat up in bed, and Ev also sat up awake.
"What's that?" Ev said.
"I don't know," I said as I climbed out of bed.

I stood at the top of the stairs and the music, which was pop music, was coming from down stairs.

I walked down the stairs. Over the top of every interior door in the house is a small glass pane, and as I came down the stairs I could see through the glass the colours of the television flickering.

We have a cockatiel and a cat, so the living room door is always locked by a chain. I unlocked the chain and walked in. The television was on *MTV*, one of Lee's favourites.

I turned around and there stood Ev, Natasha and Craig.

I said, "It must have been the timer," switching the television off, but knowing full well that no one had ever used the timer on the television.

I locked the door again, saw everyone to bed, and then settled down.

Suddenly, as my head touched the pillow there it was again.

We all met on top of the stairs and I went down again, this time on my own. I stood there after switching the television off again and said, "I know you're here son."

I sat there by the television and once again in the dark I could smell that same sweet heady smell from the Chapel of Rest.

I stood up and said, "Enough now, let the kids sleep okay? We know you're here."

Another time I was in the bathroom brushing my teeth; Natasha and Ev were in bed and Craig was already asleep.

I distinctly heard Lee call out, '*Mum, mum,*' from the bottom of the stairs.

I walked out of the bathroom and Natasha stood there in her nightie and Ev came out the bedroom. Craig was quietly snoring. Ev looked at me, so did Tash, nothing was said and we all went back to bed.

The next day I was in the living room and was heading towards the telephone in the hallway, when I heard 'Ding-Ding-Ding-Ding.'

It was coming from the kitchen and as I entered, I could see the light inside the microwave going on and off and it was making that distinctive ding sound as it had switched off. Then suddenly it started again, just for a second, before it went ding again. I had to unplug it.

That night as I was dozing I felt the quilt on top of us begin to slowly slide down.

I said to Evelyn, "What are you doing?"

Ev sat up rubbing her eyes, and we both saw the quilt move slowly down the bed and flop over the foot board at the bottom of the bed.

Ev said, "Who did that?"

I looked at Ev, "Who do you think?" Ev looked at me and said, "It slipped off on its own."

I shrugged, got out of bed, replaced the quilt on us and went back to sleep.

Shortly after this I was in the living room watching television with Ev when suddenly the lights went off in the living room.

As I stood up I could hear Craig and Natasha both shout down stairs, "Dad! The lights have gone off."

I replied: "Don't worry it's only a fuse."

I made my way to the kitchen and as I opened the kitchen door I noticed the lights where still on in there. I checked the fuse box and no switches were down. I returned to the living room and felt for the light switch; the rocker on the light switch was pushed in at the top.

I pressed the bottom of the switch and the lights in the living room came back on. I went back into the hallway and shouted, "Okay kids switch the lights back on."

I heard two clicks and I could see the lights come on upstairs.

Natasha came out of her room and said, "How did that happen Dad?"

I looked at Ev who was just staring at me.

I said to Ev, "We need to talk with the kids you know?"

Ev slowly nodded, she was getting stronger and she was receiving daily telephone calls from a service called 'Compassionate friends' and they were great, as were the Samaritans.

CHAPTER 14 – You're Roman Catholic now

I had to visit the Chapel of Rest to see about some small laminated cards being made up for the family with a beautiful poem I had asked for, to be placed on the back. It read like this:

A Poem for The Grieving

Do not stand at my grave and weep.
I am not there, I do not sleep.
I am a thousand winds that blow,
I am the diamond glints on snow.
I am the sunlight on ripened grain,
I am the gentle autumn's rain.
When you awaken in the morning's hush,
I am the swift uplifting rush
of quiet birds in circled flight.
I am the stars that shine at night.
Do not stand at my grave and cry,
I am not there, I did not die.

Myself and Ev had to see the Minister of Our Lady of Walsingham Roman Catholic Church. We met him in his office in the church; Ev explained to him that Lee had not taken his Holy Communion. He said, "My dear, before he comes into this church he will be a Roman Catholic."

We selected the hymns and asked if two songs could be played. One was obviously *Imagine*. The other one by Eric Clapton, *Tears in Heaven* as Eric had also lost his child to a fall and wrote this song about his own tragedy.

The next day I had to visit the funeral parlour again and John, as I came to know him, met me in the reception.

I explained that we had decided what we wanted on these cards (they were plastic cards like a small credit card) with a poem on it.

John handed me a small, brown envelope and said, "This ring was on your son's finger. I wondered if you would like it."

I opened the envelope and found the ring that Claire had given to Lee and said, "His girlfriend Claire bought the ring for Lee and she wanted him to keep it on."

The ring was placed back on his finger.

By now, at night in bed I was aware of people walking through my bedroom. I would see a shadow and quickly sit up and put the bedside light on in case it was one of the kids.

No one was there.

Have you ever woken up and found one of your children standing by your bed watching you sleep intently? It's a shock, isn't it?

Well that's what it was like. I would stir, wake up and look up to a woman or a man just standing by my bed, staring at me and then they were gone, just like that. Then I was seeing balls of light floating through the air like orbs and coloured balls of light too.

One night I was awoken and in the dim light from the window and the moon, I could see Nanna sitting on my bed.

She smiled and said, '*Dennis, it is time for you to use your gift sweetheart. Don't be afraid, you knew this time would come.*'

That's all she said. She leaned forward and kissed me on the cheek and then she was gone.

We made our way back to the Chapel of rest, and we each placed a rose in Lee's coffin. I wrote a letter to him and so did Ev and these too were placed in his coffin.

Craig had asked if his Man Utd cap could go in too, so we placed that in as well.

It was the day of the funeral, and everyone was at our house, relatives, Claire's family and loads of Lee's friends.

The hearse and cars turned up and we climbed in. Ev said, "I need a ciggy," knowing she couldn't have one.

We arrived at the church and it was mobbed, hundreds standing outside. Lee had friends and relatives that were going to carry him to his resting place.

I was so gutted that I could not do this last thing for him, carry him, but with my bad back and shoulder I knew I couldn't.

We climbed out of the hearse outside the church and there was Steve who had found Lee that night, Glenn, Claire's father, Wayne who went to school with Lee and Mick Jones, a long- standing family friend that Lee had known for years. Also, a great friend of mine and Lee's, Davy Tee-Boon.

They stood behind the hearse as Lee was brought out on rollers, and they hoisted him onto their shoulders like they had done it a thousand times. Their faces where serious, all trying not to make a mistake.

As they approached the church they were met by the Minister. He was standing in the vestry and had a small stick with a ball on the end and was dressed in all his regalia. He shouted, "Stop."

The lads carrying Lee stood stock still, he placed this silver orb on a handle into a vessel and sprinkled holy water on the front of the cross and bellowed loudly, "I welcome you into the Roman Catholic Church of Our Lady of Walsingham, and I bless you in the name of the Father, the Son and the holy Ghost."

He sprinkled another cross on the front of the coffin and said, "Welcome to my church, my son."

The lads carried on in and all the family sat at the front.

I could not believe that Lee was in this coffin, surrounded by candles and right next to us.

Our Ladies of Walsingham is a huge church and during the service anyone who was a Catholic and wanted to take communion could go to the front and take the bread and wine.

Those of us who were not had to cross our arms across the front of our chest, and the minister blessed us. This over, the hymns and the prayers went on.

By this time Ev had a counsellor, who was brilliant. Her name was Paula and she was from the Women's Centre in Corby. Paula sat on the other side of Ev.

Near the end of the service the minister said, "Lee's family have asked for two songs to be played, so please sit back, relax and listen to the music."

The two songs were as we had arranged. *Imagine* first, *Tears in Heaven* next.

You could hear the soft sobbing of people behind us.

As we were about to leave Ev collapsed. I had to lift her, helped by Paula, and finally she got to her feet, sobbing.

The lads raised Lee, and as before, all in step, as if they had done this a thousand times hoisted him onto their shoulders and we followed Lee out back to the hearse and then to Shire Lodge cemetery.

We all lay a rose on the coffin and, after the internment at the cemetery, we all went back to the Danesholme club where Corby Welfare Rights Services had laid on a buffet for the mourning breakfast.

Ev and I at Lee's grave

Loads of Lee's friends came back to our home after the buffet, and we talked about Lee and his antics until the early hours of the morning until finally, exhausted, I saw the last of them out.
'I will clean up tomorrow,' I thought, switched the

light out and fell exhausted into bed.

As I was sleeping I had a dream; it was like a scene from the film *Mary Poppins,* where the chimney sweep is on the rooftops of London. I could see across all the rooftops and hopping from roof top to roof top came Lee.

Then, I was back in my bedroom and in the wall next to our window a hole appeared and Lee came in through it. He sat on the bed next to me, in his favourite jacket and trousers, and said,

'I am okay Dad. Tell Mum I'm fine, okay? I love you all, you all did so well today and I will be back.'

I was just about to talk to him but he was gone, back out of the hole which closed and that was that.

I told Evelyn the next morning about my dream and she just smiled.

Hours went into days and days into weeks.

CHAPTER 15 - Evidence

I was a volunteer for Corby Welfare Rights Services and I was there one day when another volunteer, Irene, who was a great lady full of life and vigour and about seventy years of age, said, "Dennis, if Evelyn needs help and comfort tell her to go to Corby Spiritual Church.
I lost all four of my sons, and my husband, and they helped me a great deal."
I smiled and said, "Thank you."
I sat and thought, 'I remembered Nanna, and Mum before them Ray, my step Dad, used to go to Spiritual Churches but it all seemed so long ago now,' but then I also thought, 'No. Ev would say, "not likely" and that would be that.'
I arrived home about six-thirty pm and sat having my dinner, when about seven o'clock I suddenly remembered what Irene had said about the Spiritual Church.
I asked Evelyn if she would like to go, hoping she would say, 'No thanks.'
But she replied, "Oh yes, please can we?"

I was shocked to say the least.
I telephoned the Civic Centre in Corby town centre, at the Willows Complex, where I knew the Spiritual Church was.
I enquired and the man on the information desk replied, "It is on tonight at seven thirty, but you need to be here by seven fifteen to get a seat."
We quickly put on our coats and flew to the Willows complex.
We did not tell Natasha or Craig.
We arrived shortly after seven fifteen and were met at the door by a man called Tony. He shook our hands and welcomed us.
We sat and looked around and everyone seemed so friendly and welcoming.
We were singing hymns and prayers were said and all the way through this, a gentleman, who sat next to Tony, who it turned out was the Medium, sat tapping his nose, and I noticed he was continually staring at Ev.
Tony stood up and said, "Well ladies and gentlemen, it is now time for our speaker of the week, Vince Price, to allow us to hear from our loved ones as he links with the Spirit World. If he should come to you, please answer in a loud and clear voice."
Tony sat down and Vince stood up. He immediately pointed at Ev and said, "He is not going to wait, I have got to come straight to you."
Ev grabbed my hand.
Vince said, "I have a young man here in his early

twenties, blonde hair and blue eyes, he says he passed through an impact, like a crash."
Vince gestured by clapping his hands, and went on.
"He said it was very sudden, no pain. Just one second here and the next second gone. Do you understand this at all?"
I replied, "Yes, it's our son."
Vince then said, "He is showing me cars, was this a vehicle accident?" I replied, "No, but I know why he is showing you cars."
He said, "Hang on he is falling, did he pass to Spirit due to a parachute accident?"
Again, I said, "No, but you're on the right track."
"He is saying thanks for putting his ring back on him. Do you understand this?"
I said, "Oh yes, I do."
Ev by now was softly sobbing, squeezing my hand for dear life.
"You know he is near you by a fragrance you don't like, don't you?" I smiled, "Yes you're right."
"He chose to come with this fragrance because you place this directly with him."
I again replied, "Yes."
I was still not one hundred percent convinced, as I knew that this tragedy had a lot of local newspaper coverage being a suicide.
Then Vince said, "He is giving me a pain to my chest and the back of my head."
Only the police and we knew this: that Lee had gone over the edge of the multi-story car park

backwards and the impact was so great that as he landed on his shoulders, the top of his back and the back of his head, his rib cage blew apart, and he badly damaged the back of his head.
But when people asked, "Did he look all right in the chapel of rest? It said in the paper that the damage was his chest and head." Thinking he landed on the ground face down.

So, when Vince was rubbing his chest and the back of his head I knew Lee was there with him, and so did Ev. Vince then pointed to Ev and said, "You know when he is around you as he makes plants move."
Ev said through tears, "Yes, that's right."
I looked at Ev, she turned and said, "I will tell you later."
Vince then said, "He is so, so sorry. He never for a moment thought so many people would be hurt by this. He is fine, no more pain for what he was doing, and as he pulls away he says he read all your letters, and thanks for all your roses."
I sat there dumb founded. Okay, if this had happened forty years ago, when I was twelve I may have been more accepting, but my life had moved on, and I did not expect this.
Ev was by now in floods of tears, knowing that Lee had been there.
A lady named Sharon took Ev behind a screen to give her some healing.
When the service was over, Vince approached

where I was sitting and said, "Is this your first time in a Spiritual Church?"

I smiled and said, "Yes, does it show?"

Vince smiled and replied, "What's your name?"

"Dennis."

Vince then took my hand and said, "Hi Dennis, you are a Medium. How come I had to do that when you are just as well equipped as me for giving messages? You know he wants you to work for Spirit, don't you? So he can talk to his mother."

By now Ev had returned. She had no idea of my past as far as Mediumship and Clairvoyance went. Vince smiled and said to Ev, "Thank you for allowing me to work with you and your son."

Ev smiled in reply and we left for home.

On the way, I said, "What do you think?"

Ev said, "Lee was definitely there. That Medium couldn't know all that, could he?" Ev turned to look at me searching.

"No love. He certainly wouldn't," I replied.

Ev kept going over and over the details Vince had given us.

CHAPTER 16 – Dad. It's me

We arrived home and went to bed.
I couldn't sleep and decided to see if an hour on the computer would help tire me. I was soon surfing, when I suddenly had an idea, I typed in 'Spiritual and Psychic sites' and several web pages appeared on my monitor.
I looked at one which read 'Free Psychic readings in our chat rooms.' I decided to check this one out and found myself on a site called www.psychics.co.uk. I entered a chat room for Spiritual readings and I sat for about an hour watching people from all over the world chatting, mainly about their experiences of the people they had lost.
Then, a lady named Blue Angel put up on the screen 'I have a young man here, he is around early twenties, very good looking, blonde hair, blue eyes. He says a tragic passing.'
I sat there looking at the screen 'It couldn't be surely,' I thought.
She continued to type, 'He gives me an L name and is looking for his Mum and Dad.'

No one answered, so I typed 'I think I know him.'
She typed, 'Who is Dennis?'
I froze.
I looked around the room and with a dry mouth I replied, 'I am.'
She then said, 'Did he pass to Spirit due to a fall?'
I sat back. It was Lee.
I replied, 'Yes.'
She went on to say, 'He says, for some reason, he has spoken to you tonight already.'
I smiled and shouted, "Ev, Ev it's Lee, he is here."
Ev sat up, wide eyed.
She looked at me angrily but before she could get a word out I said, "On here look, he is here."
Ev pulled a chair up and said, "What are you talking about? How can he be on a computer?"
I said, "I really don't know how but he is here, look read."
I scrolled back the page.
I said to Blue Angel, 'Where are you? Are you in the UK?'
'No NYC.'
I gulped and said to Ev, "She is American and in New York City."
"Why would Lee go all the way to New York City?" she asked.
I sat there thinking, remembering my days back with my grandmother.
"They will use anything to communicate, anything and this is a way of communication."
Blue Angel went on, 'He says his mum is finding it

difficult to accept he is alive, that he is there right now with you.'

Ev said, "Well I am sorry Dennis but look around, we are the only ones here."

She went to stand up when Blue Angel wrote, 'Why is he amongst cars? He says there were cars and he fell on his back.'

Ev gulped, pulled her nightie tighter around her and climbed back into bed. Blue Angel then said, 'He is pulling away, but says he is going to give his mother the proof she needs, irrefutable proof. I am sorry, he has pulled away.'

I thanked her many times.

I found this amazing and so fulfilling to me, I knew it was Lee, but I looked over to the bed and Ev was already under the covers.

I switched off the computer, and went for a drink of water for my medication. I returned, took a book and climbed in bed next to Ev; I was reading for about 10 minutes.

We have two wardrobes, his and hers with a mirrored dressing table in-between, (the very one I looked into when Lee blew on my neck). We sometimes hang jeans or t-shirts over the door so they are ajar.

I was reading when Ev's wardrobe door made a creaking noise and slowly shut. I looked, thinking it was Liquorice, our cat, climb into our wardrobe. Then slowly it opened, nothing was inside, no cats or dogs, and then the door of my wardrobe opened and closed and then the door of her

wardrobe opened but a bit quicker.
Suddenly, all four doors, two of Ev's wardrobe and two of mine began opening and closing with such speed, they were banging, then they became louder and louder.
By now they were flying open and closed, banging and crashing, the wardrobes where rocking and dust was flying off the top of them, old pen tops and pieces of games and jigsaw's also.
Ev sat up and over the noise shouted, "What is going on?"
I was sat up, reading, as if this was normal and said, "What do you mean? That?" Pointing to the doors which were now sounding like a machine gun, rhythmically opening and shutting.
I said, "Oh that, it's Lee giving you evidence he is here."
Ev sat staring, unbelievably, but then her face lit up and smiled, she sat up in bed, and clasped her hands together, "Go on Lee," she shouted, "bang those doors."
I looked around and Natasha and Craig were at our bedroom door, looking wide eyed and open mouthed.
Natasha said, "Lee?" Pointing to the doors, the racket was deafening.
I smiled and climbed out of bed, I said, "Don't be scared kids okay? He has a point to prove," I looked at Ev and said, "doesn't he?"
But Ev was in a world of her own, smiling, looking at the phenomena taking place in front of us all.

Slowly she nodded, and said, "Yes." Almost as if Lee had been waiting for his mum's recognition that it was him the doors slowly came to a standstill, still rocking a little, but slower and slower and then to a standstill.
"Want to kip in here kids?" I asked and they both jumped in our bed, and we all went to sleep.

By now I was exhausted, I was having lights moving around the room, people walking through the room and I was hearing voices.
Lee was calling out in the middle of the night; my computer would suddenly whirl into action and again the television was switching on and off.

I decided one Sunday to go to another Spiritual Church in Corby known as Kelvin Grove; the service was on Sunday at 3pm.
I arrived and sat through it which was beautiful. At the end of the service I was talking to people, some of whom knew Lee, and what had taken place. I explained some of the phenomena that was taking place in my home, when a lady named Linda said, "I know a lady who may be able to help you. Her name is Lynn and she lives in Kettering." She handed me a piece of paper with a telephone number on it.

CHAPTER 17 - Lynn

I arrived home about 6pm, and explained to Ev what the lady at the Church had said.
I telephoned the name on the piece of paper: Lynn Cottrell.
A lady answered and I said, "Hello my name is Dennis. My son died about four months ago, and I am having some really weird things happen in my home."
"What type of things Dennis?"
I explained all that was going on.
"That is just Lee trying desperately to contact you, it must be for a reason, what about if I came out to visit you and Evelyn?"
I was really pleased.
Lynn said, "I will be able to call on Tuesday at 2pm, is that okay?" I agreed. That afternoon I walked into the kitchen and as I passed the knife and fork draw it flew open with such a force that the knives and forks came flying out all over the floor. I bent down to pick them up, and I was aware of someone behind me. I turned around

and I saw Lee, standing there in one of his favourite zip up boxer jackets and dark blue trousers. He smiled and put his thumb up and then he was gone. Just like that. This is what he wanted.

On Tuesday afternoon, there was a knock on the door and a young lady, about thirty-five, with blonde hair and a brief case stood there.

"Hello, are you Dennis?"

You must remember, I had a shaven head, a goatee beard and a moustache and although I was suffering terribly with arthritis, I had still retained a lot of my muscle mass from years of training, and I looked as you would expect a night club bouncer to look.

I invited Lynn in and introduced her to Evelyn.

Lynn took one look at me and said, "My dear, you are wide open to Spirit. We have to close you up a little; no wonder all this is going on."

Lynn spoke to me in detail and she then explained that through grief I was opening myself to Spirit, and that I had a very strong ability for Spirit work. Lynn left and I agreed to go to her development circle the following Monday.

I then sat and explained to Ev about my mother and grandmother and all the goings on at 113 Carrasbrook Road, Liverpool.

Ev sat there, gob smacked, mouth wide open, "Why didn't you ever tell me Dennis?"

I explained that it was so very long ago and that I had not really been aware of my Psychic ability or any Mediumship since joining the Army, except for a couple of times.

Straight away things began to stop happening from that afternoon. I slept throughout the night for the first time in many months.

On Monday evening I arrived at Lynn's home. I knocked the door, and Lynn answered. She gave me a big hug and I followed her into the living room where about twelve to fourteen people sat in a circle.

I found an empty chair and Lynn introduced me. Everyone seemed very friendly and I immediately felt welcome and relaxed. Lynn explained meditating and the safety of it to protect one's self. She asked us all to sit quiet and relaxed and said "Dear heavenly Father, please bring close all our helpers, inspirer's and guides from the Spirit World and allow these people who sit in this circle of light, truth and knowledge to be instruments for Spirit, and please surround every member of this circle, my family and my home with your beautiful, white, protective light, Amen."

We all looked up, I remembered my grandmother's circles, but this one seemed more relaxed, people were laughing and talking, it was great. Lynn explained that we would be doing some psychic exercises. She picked up a pack of Angel cards, and gave one to each of us. Lynn then asked us to concentrate, hold the card in the palm of each hand, as if you were praying with the Angel card between your palms, and then send your

thoughts to it. Just be aware of the card.
After a couple of minutes, Lynn then asked us to turn to the right and left so we were now all facing a partner, we then swapped cards.
Lynn asked us to allow the card to guide us. "Do not look at the value of the card or the writing. Look through the card, but be aware of it, and allow your gut feelings, any hunches, it may be as light as a tiny snow flake passing by, but grab it. Okay, begin."
I said to the lady facing me, "Who's going to go first?"
The lady, named Kate, said, "It's Dennis, isn't it? You can go first, okay?"
I relaxed, brought myself together, and just became aware of the card, looking at it, but through the colours and images I said, "I am being shown someone having to use a new jack on a car."
Kate smiled and said, "My husband went to a car boot yesterday and came back with some books and a car jack. He had to change the wheels around to allow even wear."
I smiled too, my confidence picking up. I again looked at the swirl of colours and I was aware of a cherub like statue. I said to Kate, "I am seeing like a white porcelain figure of a baby or a cherub laying on a sheet or a blanket."
Kate replied, "I have ordered two from a magazine, you know you see things like plaques, and jewellery being advertised in these Sunday

magazines?"

I said, "Okay, your turn."

Kate smiled and looked deep into my card, "I am being made aware of a sudden realisation, like a door opening for you, one you kept closed for many years."

I said, "Wow! Yes, you're smack on." Kate smiled and wriggled in her chair, as if she was settling down now that she had scored a good hit.

"You need a new television. Yours keeps going on and off."

I couldn't help laughing, and everyone stopped and looked at me. I felt such a fool.

Lynn came over as she was slowly going around everyone.

Lynn said, smiling, "Everything okay? What happened?"

"Well, Kate does not know this but I have had loads of phenomena happening in my home and one of them is my television going on and off all night."

Kate smiled, with her mouth open and put her hand over her mouth.

"I would never have believed it," Lynn said, "Well done Kate. How did Dennis get on?"

Kate explained what I had said and confirmed the reading.

Lynn said, "Well done Dennis, that is good stuff on your first day; I expect a lot from you."

Smiling, I just hunched my shoulders as if to say, 'I hope so.'

The rest of the evening was spent doing various Psychic exercises, and I surprised myself with my accuracy. After three weeks of sitting in Circle, Lynn said, after the meditation, "I want to try some linking with Spirit."

Lynn went on to pair us up. I was with Allen, a Scottish guy also from Corby.

"You go first Dennis," Lynn said.

I sat for a moment and slowly took myself back to when I was twelve years of age, standing in a circle. I was suddenly aware of a young lady, aged about forty-five. I said to Allen, "I am aware of a lady. She is not old, around forty-five years of age. She has a kind of beret on her head and she has jet black hair. A very pretty lady, standing holding a bike, in a white dress with black poker dots on it and black gloves. Does this make sense?"

Allen was looking at me with his eyes wide open. He was about sixty-three years of age, he said, "That's my ma."

"Okay, she is taking me to her lungs and says 'TB.'"

Allen said, "Oh my God! She passed with tuberculosis. I will bring a photograph in for you next week Dennis. It is my ma, just as you described her."

The rest of the readings gathered up in pace and evidence. At one stage I was aware of Lynn standing behind me, her hand to her chin, listening intently.

At the end of the evening, as we were leaving, Lynn said, "Dennis, wait here for a minute, I want to talk to you."

I sat down again and Lynn sat next to me and said, "The evidence you're giving is remarkable, only now and again does someone enter a circle like you. Have you done this before?"

I explained about my childhood and my experiences with my mother and grandmother. Lynn sat listening carefully as I went through the tragic passing of Lee, and all the things going on at home, which she was already aware of from her visit. I could not explain in detail as Ev was listening. Lynn sat for a moment and said, "You have a rare gift Dennis, and I would like you to accompany me on my next Church service. You don't have to do anything, just sit in the energy and see how you feel."

I said, "That would be great, thank you very much."

I told Evelyn everything that went on in the Circle and she sat pensively listening. I still had not really let out my grief from the passing of Lee, even though every day if we wanted to visit the town centre we had to pass the bus station where Lee had fallen.

I was still stuck in between screaming and crying, so nothing happened.

I went to see my doctor in the end who sent me to the practice councillor; we talked and talked and then it happened. It seemed easier with a stranger. I cried and cried, and cried some more.

"I am ever so sorry," I said.
He smiled, "This is what should have happened. I am glad it did, it has released some feelings."
I went home with a weight off my chest.

CHAPTER 18 - Elmer Street

On Monday night about 5.30pm, Lynn called, and we set off for Grantham Spiritualist Church.

Lynn said, as we were travelling, "Don't worry if you don't pick up anything Dennis. I just want you to sit in the energy tonight, but if you do think you have something for one of the congregation, let me know. Okay?"

I just nodded. I knew that Nanna was with me, I could smell her lavender perfume, and I could hear her talking to me, *'Remember what we did when you were a laa, okay? Just take your mind to that comfortable place, and I will be there.'* She was gone.

In no time at all we arrived in Grantham and pulled up in Elmer Street. A lady met us and Lynn asked if I could help her with her equipment. Lynn is what is known as a 'Psychic Artist' in that she can draw a very distinctive likeness of a loved one in Spirit, so I helped her with an easel, pastel chalks, charcoal, and pencils.

The lady who was the President of the Church asked if we would like some quiet time as we had twenty-five minutes before the service began, so Lynn and myself sat in a small room, which I learned later was a healing room.

It had beautiful pictures on the walls, and some incense sticks burning. I sat and lowered myself into meditation; I was aware of the familiar feeling of a tight band around my forehead and I could see Dancing Rain sitting cross legged opposite me. He said, *'From here,'* pointing to his forehead, *'look from here, when you are ready I will help you.'* I was aware of my grandmother again, she looked as she did when I was in Liverpool, like Gloria Swanson again.

She walked over to me, brushed my lapels as if they were dusty, she licked a handkerchief and rubbed the side of my face. I could smell her strong lipstick from the handkerchief as I did when I was a child, *You look at me Dennis Binks, this is where you are meant to be son. You will be fine.'*

And then I heard Lynn gently saying, "Dennis, are you ready?"

I slowly opened my eyes, Lynn asked, "Would you like a drink of water first?"

I just shook my head and said, "No thanks, I am fine." And with that the lady chairperson opened the door.

The church was packed, as Lynn was well known for her Psychic Art. We walked to the platform and sat down.

I don't remember much about the beginning of

the service. You see as soon as I sat down there was a young girl, about nineteen, sitting about three rows back on the left. She had a baby in the crook of her left arm, but I was also seeing a baby in the crook of her right arm too, except I knew that the baby in her right arm was in Spirit.

Lynn stood up and said, "Well, Dennis is what we term as a fledgling or I prefer a novice Medium, now Dennis may not pick anything up tonight." Lynn turned and looked at me, she stopped and looked in the direction I was looking, "Dennis, are you picking anything up?"

I just nodded, and then said, "Can I talk to the young lady there?"

Lynn said, "Of course you can."

Just then I was aware of an elderly gentleman, about seventy years of age, quite tall, about six foot, a full head of wavy hair brushed back. He walked close to this young lady and the babies.

He said, *'This is my granddaughter's friend, and the baby you are seeing is Natalie. Natalie is my great granddaughter, she passed over to us at three months of age.*

Please ask this young lady to let my granddaughter know that Natalie is fine and with me. Natalie had a tummy problem with her bowels.'

All this information had flashed in a split second through my mind, I coughed and sent him a thought, *Okay my friend, let's do this.'*

He smiled and I said, "I want to talk to you, my love." Pointing to the young lady holding the baby.

"Who me?" she said, looking around. "Yes, I have an elderly gentleman here that says you're a friend of someone who lost a little girl at the age of three months old. The baby was named Natalie."

The young lady gasped, and looked wide eyed, "Yes," was all she could say.

I then went on, "Please tell her that Natalie is with her great grandfather and is fine."

The young lady smiled and said, "I will. She was supposed to come tonight but could not make it. Thank you"

I sat down and Lynn said, "Well done Dennis."

Lynn was just about to say something else when a dove flew in the room, I knew this also was from Spirit as no one else was looking at it as it flew slowly over the heads of the congregation.

It hovered for a moment over a lady. It seemed to go into slow motion and had a white aura surrounding it.

I said, "Lynn, can you see that dove, over there?"

Lynn stared in the direction I was pointing and said, "No."

I smiled and said, "I have another one then."

"Okay sweetheart, you knock 'em out." The dove settled on the ground and sat by an elderly lady. Suddenly, another elderly lady appeared next to her. She said, *'Joan, Joan Dove."* I replied, *'I want to come to you please.'*

The elderly lady whispered, *Bless you.'*

I said, "Would you understand the name Dove?"

She looked at me, shocked and said, "My name's Dove."

"So, who is Joan then?" I asked.

Her eyes filled with tears and she said, "That is my mother."

Joan looked at me and I was aware of having difficulty in breathing slightly. I was also aware all at once of an oxygen mask, an inhaler, and a nebuliser. I recognised these things as my stepfather had all these with his emphysema.

I then said, "This lady is taking me to my chest and this looks and feels like emphysema."

The lady replied, "Yes, that's right. She died of emphysema and she had oxygen bottles in her bedroom."

Joan then tugged at my ring on my finger. I had a gold band on, a wedding ring from Evelyn.

"Your mother is tugging this ring on my finger."

The lady then held up her hand and there was a wedding band.

Joan then said, *Tell her to sell that bloody awful house.*"

I gulped, looked at Lynn and turned again, "Your mother is saying, 'sell that bloody awful house.'"

Everyone started laughing.

Lynn stood up and coughed.

The lady I was giving the message to was also laughing and said, "Yes, she hated her house, and said before she passed away, 'do me a favour, get rid of this.'"

Joan blew me a kiss and I sat down. I felt really

happy, I was so pleased that it had worked.

Lynn stood up and said, "Well done Dennis, that was wonderful. Don't you all think so?"

They all applauded. I just smiled awkwardly and nodded in thanks.

Lynn then did some fantastic drawings. I was intrigued at the amount of information that also came through with her drawings.

This was my first service and I felt champagne corks popping behind me and a whisper from Dancing Rain, *We still have a long way to go. No champagne for you.'* I smiled, I knew he was a hard task master.

CHAPTER 19 - Stansted

I arrived home at about ten-thirty. Evelyn was in the front room watching television and the kids where in bed, "How did it go, Den?" she asked, getting up.
I stood there for a moment, finding it hard to explain this amazing phenomena.
I slowly took my coat off and sat down.
"I don't know how to explain it; it's like they come from heaven to talk. You know they are there, it is so much stronger when you are in a place like a Spiritual Church."
Ev took my coat and said, "Was Lee with you?"
"He may have been sweetheart, but I didn't see or feel him around me." Ev took my coat out and hung it up. I heard her put the kettle on. This was so hard, developing this ability as well as grieving. And there was Ev, she found this hard as well.

As the weeks went by I found my ability becoming stronger.
One day Lynn said, "You need Stansted now

Dennis".
"Stansted? What is that?"
"The Arthur Findlay College near Stansted, for Spiritual and Psychic Awareness. You would love it, I know." She handed me a book about the college.

One night, there was a film on the television which was about a lad who had taken his own life. I glanced at Ev and I could see tears running down her cheeks.
Slowly, a figure appeared before me, I recognised the side view of this person, it was Lee. He was in a short-sleeved shirt and a pair of tan coloured trousers, his blonde hair swept back.
He walked over to his mother, who was oblivious of him being here. I saw him cup his hands under her eyes. He looked at me, and I could see him properly now, like he had never gone. *'I am catching Mum's tears Daa."*
I said, "Lee's here Ev, he said...." And before I could finish Ev turned to me, her face wet with tears, and she screamed, "Don't you understand it? I don't want Lee's Spirit. I want my Lee back here, don't keep on about his Spirit. I want him. Is that so hard to understand?"
This snapped me back to earth and she dropped her head into her hands and sobbed.
Lee was gone just like that.
I ran over to her and hugged her and said, "I'm sorry Ev I didn't think. I was trying to let you know

he was here that's all."

Ev wiped her tears and her nose and sat up, regaining her composure a bit. "I know, it is just so hard Dennis. I know you see him and I know he talks to you."

Bingo. I knew what the trouble was, of course. I could see Lee and he talked to me. Ev, his own mother, had not sensed him around her at all. But thousands of people lose loved ones and never sense them, but then again, they don't have some guy jumping around the place talking to them either.

Ev went to bed, and I sat in my usual chair in the kitchen where I meditate. I closed my eyes, it was so quiet, and slowly I slid deeper and deeper.

I could hear a loud rattle being shaken, but this was no baby's rattle. It sounded heavy. I was aware of looking down at my feet and seeing I had my old army boots on, and as I looked up I checked my clothing. I was wearing my camouflage uniform and a beret on my head.

I looked around and down a slope were many tee-pees all with their sticks out the top, various colours but mainly the fawn colour of animal skin. I could then smell wood burning, and I slowly began to walk down, with the sound of this rattle I could also hear a drum beat, it had two different sounds, one heavy and one light. There was a fog or a mist, but as I walked closer I began to see figures come into view.

They were Native Americans. One had long raven

black hair pulled back and held in place with some decorated bones, he had a red pair of baggy trousers with frills at the side. I heard them singing and then I could see the fire, a huge bonfire crackling away, and sitting around it where many Native Americans, in different arrays of clothing and feathers.

I was then aware of someone next to me. I turned and there smiling, was Dancing Rain. He was in full regalia, a huge head dress, and wearing buck skins which had different coloured beads attached. He was so tall, he must have been six foot six inches at least and very broad, but he had a kind face and a warm and knowing look about him. He said, *'Come with me.'*

He began to walk around the outside of the area and we went right around to the other side. I could feel the heat of the fire on my face, and I could hear the whooping and singing of the many Native Americans, who sat around the fire cross legged, their long black hair pulled back and tied at the back.

Some had blankets wrapped around them. They had brown faces, very craggy and wrinkled due to many winters, I guess. As soon as they saw me, their eyes lit up, dark brown eyes, that seemed so full of knowledge and feelings.

They began to talk to me, but I couldn't understand a word. One of them jumped up and handed me a set of coloured beads. He pointed to his throat, bowed, smiled and walked away back to where he was sitting.

I looked down at the beads, and I could hear an eagle screaming above me. Dancing Rain walked up to another Native Indian, and began to talk in a language I did not understand. This other Indian had a more serious look about him than Dancing Rain. He had a raccoon on his head, and the back of the raccoon was down his back; he also had some white paint on his face. He was about fifty to sixty years of age and again tall and broad.

He bent down to the fire where I observed a bowl with some weird looking liquid in it and it was bubbling away as the fire was so hot. The Native American who was tending to this, picked up a small wooden bowl and tipped some of the liquid in it. I couldn't see the colour for the steam and smoke. He turned and looked at me. I gulped as I guessed what was to follow.

He walked up to me, handed me the bowl and pointed to his mouth. I looked at Dancing Rain, who smiled and pointed to his mouth, so I placed the bowl to my lips and took a sip.

Dancing Rain who stepped forward and said, '*We are warriors, you are a warrior too.*'

I said, "Yeah, but that was a long time ago."

Dancing Rain placed a finger to his lips and then said, '*For this job, that you have to do, you need to be a warrior, not with a gun, but with your heart and soul, for you will cry, you will pain, this is not an easy task. Do you want it still?*'

I smiled, and said, "More than anything."

Dancing Rain smiled and turned to the others sitting round the fire and he let out a blood curdling yell. Suddenly, they all stood up and started shouting and screaming. Their faces with different paint covering them, some with blue and red marks, others half black and white. Dancing Rain turned and shouted over the noise, which was deafening, *'Now it begins.'*

Bang! I was sitting in the chair in the kitchen again, with just the sound of the clock ticking.

'What was that all about?' I thought. I swallowed and I could taste a funny taste in my mouth. I walked over to the sink and spat into it.

Red liquid came out of my mouth and I thought for a moment it was blood, but it had a different consistency to blood, it was lighter in colour, and it tasted of herbs.

I swilled my mouth out with water and brushed my teeth. I thought about my recent meditation and the words, 'Now it begins.'

Evelyn was asleep when I climbed into bed.

I had difficulty getting off to sleep but in the end I slowly slid into a deep sleep and in the darkness of my sleep I could hear someone calling, I could not make out what it was but I could hear a voice, and slowly it grew clearer: *'Dad, daa.'*

I found myself sitting on a bench in a park, with huge trees around me, and as I turned to the right I could see Lee walking up to me. He had a dark blue jacket on and some tan trousers with an open neck shirt. He jumped over the back of the bench and sat by my side. I just stared at him with my mouth open, looking at him up and down. I couldn't take it all in.

'Dad,' he said again, this time loud in my face, *'it's me, Lee. Come on man. I haven't got all day.'*

I looked around and just looked him up and down again. I touched his arm, and placed my hand on his, it was soft and warm and I could feel his bones underneath.

Suddenly, I could smell that familiar aftershave. I looked into his huge blue eyes; he smiled again and said, *Here you are, you see, I am okay. That stuff they give you will help.'*

I put my hand to my lips, 'That stuff?' He meant that drink.

"You mean that drink?" Suddenly the wind picked up and grass and leaves where whirling around us, Lee had to shout above the noise of the wind, *'Yes Dad, it will help you.'*

"Help me what?" I yelled.

'You'll see,' Lee said, he leaned forward and kissed me on the cheek. It was soft, wet and warm. He whispered, *'I am so, so sorry.'*

I pulled my head back so I could see Lee's face and I could see the pain in his eyes, "I know son." I screamed, but the wind was roaring and the alarm went off. It was morning, time for Craig's school.

I climbed out of bed, and Ev said, "What's that in your hair?" She reached up and about three brown leaves were in her hand.

I looked at the pillow and I could see some smaller

crushed leaves. "Where on earth did they come from?" she asked. I replied, "You ain't going to believe this."

Ev frowned and said, "Try me."

I explained all about the Native American camp, the dream with Lee, and Ev then said, "You're right, I don't know what's going on." And turned away.

I had such difficulty explaining the things that were happening to me, I tried, but she had a job handling them.

As time went on, I was travelling to Spiritual Churches all around the Midlands, my evidence of the Spirit World grew stronger and stronger.

CHAPTER 20 - Denmark

The halls and churches were gathering in numbers every time I was serving them.
I was being aware of evidence that was breathtaking even to people that had attended many Spiritual venues. At home I was talking to Lynn on the telephone when she said, "Why don't you start a circle? You used to be an instructor in the armed forces. I'm sure you could manage a circle." I thought of what Lynn said and as soon as I mentioned it to the Angels of Light Church in Corby I had a front room full of people. It came as second nature; after all methods of instruction can be applied to any subject.
I had to start taking names on a list as the circle was full. At the same time, I applied to go back to the Arthur Findlay College to refresh my teaching skills.
It was while I was there I met a young lady named Fouzia. There were other classes being taken there and we had to carry out what we had been taught

and teach a class now and then in a lesson.

Dennis Binks – stage medium

It was after one of these lessons that Fouzia approached me. She said that she came from Copenhagen and that there was a group of them there that needed a teacher to take them on a week's course of Mediumship. That they needed a good teacher. Without thinking, I said, "Okay."

Fouzia took my mobile number and said, "You will be able to stay at Miller's apartment, okay?"

I continued with the course and then returned home; my batteries now fully charged and raring to go.

It was about twelve months later I was at Rushden in Northamptonshire, where my mother lives, that my mobile rang. I answered and heard, "Hello Dennis. This is Fouzia here, we are all set up now. Sorry about the delay."

I thought back and said, "Oh hi. I had forgotten all about this."

Fouzia gave me some dates and I agreed to go to Copenhagen. I flew by Easyjet and landed in Copenhagen. I was met by Fouzia, and she gave me a hug and said, "Welcome to Copenhagen. Come on, I will take you to Millers."

I collected my luggage and off we went. As we drove through the busy streets of Copenhagen it was a beautiful sight, so many churches and old buildings, but with character. We pulled up at the apartment, and Fouzia said, "You will like Miller. She is a great friend of mine." I froze. "She?"

Fouzia looked up and said, "Yes. Why?"

At this point, Miller opened the door to her apartment and there stood a Kim Basinger look-alike.

I thought, 'Ev will never believe this.'

Miller opened her arms and grabbed me and said in broken English, "Hello Dennis, welcome to my home. I am Miller."

I said that in the UK Miller is a guy's name.

She looked strangely at me and Fouzia said, "Oh! It is Mille or in English, Millie. We pronounce it Miller."

Well, it was eleven-thirty at night and I was exhausted so in I went. Mille, as it is spelt in Danish, showed me to my room.

"You can sleep in here Dennis. It is comfy and here is the toilet," opening a door.

"Kitchen is there," pointing to another door, "and I sleep right down the hall."

It all seemed quite normal to these girls but, of course, with the British stiff upper lip we have, it felt well, not good.

I must admit Mille was a lady and after a couple of days I felt better. The week's course was eye opening as they had been taught so much rubbish. Whoever tutored these guys in ways of Spiritual and Psychic awareness had done so with fear. When there is a lack of knowledge the gap is filled with fear and jealousy.

'I have it, you're not going to have it,' attitude.

After a week, they were all linking beautifully, working with auras, and colour, and then slowly moved onto Psychic ability and linking with Spirit. Slowly their links grew stronger.

I coaxed and coaxed, watching their confidence grow and then all were giving beautiful messages.

I then moved them onto a make-shift platform where they practised ready for any services they may be asked to attend. The word had got about to their friends and family, so, the day before I left they put on a full Divine service.

It was a pleasure to watch all my hard work unfold. The room was packed. I fought back tears as I watched, first the opening prayer, which went well, a bit quick I thought, but that was nerves and then one of them did an amazing reading. This was followed by the address of fifteen minutes of good philosophy. Then it was time and one by one I watched them deliver wonderful messages.

It was a huge success; Spirit had not let us down.

I had to dash to the airport and I was swamped with hugs and whisked away through Copenhagen again to the airport. I thought, I hadn't even seen outside of the class room since arriving but that was the job. I had worked hard for this group.

CHAPTER 21 – Britain's Psychic Challenge

Back in Britain I pulled up outside my home in Corby and there was Ev waiting.
She said, "Well, how did it go?"
I took a deep breath and explained about Miller or Millie, but knowing how much my Spirit work means to me we both fell about laughing.
"You thought it was like Miller then?"
"Yes," I said, "who would have thought 'Miller' was a female?"
Ev looked at me and said, "If it wasn't so funny I would kick your butt." We both laughed.
I knew that I was meant now to teach. I found it inspiring to see students go daily from strength to strength, to teach them from the heart.

In November 2004, I was doing an evening of clairvoyance in a hall just outside Kempston, Bedfordshire.
I arrived and there were about two hundred and

fifty people there. It was about 7pm and the demonstration was to start at seven-thirty.

On the dot, the lady organising the event, which was for charity, introduced me, and onto the stage I walked.

As I was explaining to the audience how I worked, I heard a voice from somewhere in the middle of the congregation say, "Oh no, not another night of this."

I thought it was one of my friends having a laugh. I shaded my eyes from the bright lights by placing my hand over them, I smiled and said, "I beg your pardon?"

Again, the man spoke up and said, "I hope you're better than the last few we have seen."

I smiled and said, "Well how about something different then? What if I was to be blindfolded and not be able to hear any of your voices? Just have someone stand next to me and answer yes or no for you all. This means you cannot say a word, if you understand the evidence being given then put up your hand and I will ask Barbara, the organiser, if she would kindly do the honours of answering for you."

There was a lot of chatting going on, and Barbara stood on stage and said, "Would you like to see Dennis and his Spirit friends demonstrate this way?"

There was a huge cheer, "First," I said, "I will need a blindfold or a thick scarf."

Sure enough a thick, long, black scarf was handed

to me. "Now I would like two members of the audience to make sure that this is tight and secure."
Two ladies came up on stage and I handed them the scarf and it was tied securely, I couldn't see a thing. Slowly, a hush went around the huge hall and I began to give link after link. There were loud rounds of applause and soon the ninety minutes were over.
When the blindfold came off, I had a job to see, but the whole hall was standing up, person after person came up to the edge of the stage saying, "Never seen anything like it, amazing." And "That was awesome, thanks so much." And the "I'm the guy who gave you a hard time. We see so many and they are rubbish really, but you are the real thing," and he shook my hand.
I drove home and thanked Spirit for their help that evening.

The next day I was sitting at my computer desk when the telephone rang, it was a Monday morning in January 2005.
I heard a voice, very British, say, "Hello, is this Dennis Binks?"
I replied it was, the man then went on, "My name is John Vaal and I have paid through your website for a telephone reading."
"Okay Mr Vaal, or do you prefer John?"
"John, please," he replied.
I was suddenly taken to Holland, tulips and

windmills. He was calling me via a Skype phone number, so there was no way of knowing where he was calling from.

"Are you a Dutch man John?"

"Very good, yes I am Dennis."

I then said, "Your father was named John also, it is he that is here with me now."

"Yes Dennis, that's right. His name was John."

I was aware of the Dutch Resistance fighting German troops and I relayed this to John who confirmed his father was in the Resistance. I was then shown a map and a red cross on the German side of a Dutch and German border.

"You are moving to Germany John?"

"No Dennis, not me. I have no intentions of moving to Germany."

I was also shown a house that was like a small chapel, I relayed this also to John which he refuted. He denied all knowledge of moving and was so against moving anywhere.

I was then shown the earth, around his new home in Germany. All the pipes surrounding his house to take away the rain water were broken and not connected. I informed John who was now answering condescendingly and with no conviction.

"This is serious John, you need to take heed," I said. At that John thanked me and hung up.

It was 2007 and most of the UK had endured the worst flooding in recent history. I was again at my computer when the telephone rang and a man's voice said, "Hello, this is John Vaal. Do you remember me?"

I said, "No," as I didn't recognise his voice.

He explained I had given him a reading two years before and he went on to mention the house in Germany.

I said, "I do that many readings, I am sorry but I don't remember."

To which John replied, "Hang on a minute, this might help."

He had recorded the reading on his hard drive and he played it back. I sat back and heard the reading I had given two years earlier.

"Well Dennis," John said, "I did move to Germany and the house does look like a chapel and I am now talking to you from my front room, up to my ankles in water."

"Okay," I replied.

He continued, "I got an engineer to come and survey the property and he managed to x-ray the ground around the house. None of the pipe work for rain water is connected. In British money, we're looking at about eleven thousand pounds to repair all of this."

"Oh dear. You should have listened to your Father," I replied.

I got talking to John more and more over the months and in 2008, Ev and I flew to Germany and spent a week with John and his beautiful family.

It was so weird standing on the ground that I had predicted all those years ago, would flood and we remain good friends today.

I still loved demonstrating in halls, Spiritual Churches, anywhere. I remember going to one home of a young lady who had 'phoned for a reading. It was on an estate not far from where I lived.

I entered the house and met a young lady about nineteen years of age, along with her mother and they both welcomed me.

I was already aware of a young man, about twenty years of age, around me. He was a typical lad, cocky, arrogant and with a 'I don't care' attitude. He was about six feet tall, very slim with a type of Asian or Italian colour about him. He had jet black hair, short, but wavy and beautiful white teeth.

I set up my tape recorder and as I pressed the button of the recorder I explained that I was aware of this lad and what he looked like, the young girl sat forward on her chair, tears already in her eyes.

I linked with him and he said, *'Where is our baby boy? He is usually in here in the afternoon.'*

I relayed this to the young girl who placed a hand to her mouth and looked at her mother. (I always tell people to remove any photographs or anything that may lead to a person in Spirit), the lad then went on a ramble, not making sense. I remember Lee being like this, he suddenly looked pale and anxious.

I said, "This lad was into drugs, wasn't he?" The girl slowly nodded her head.

He impressed me with a vision of him lying on the grass with the girl lying across him and writing her name on his stomach 'Tanya.'

I told her what I had seen; she shot off the chair and flew upstairs. I sat waiting and when she came back down with a photograph there he was, topless, with her name 'Tanya' tattooed on his stomach.

"Wow!" she said, "I can't believe that."

He was standing beside her now and I knew what he wanted. I said, "He wants to say he is so sorry, he was stupid." The girl began to slowly sob.

"This was a drug overdose my dear, wasn't it?"

She looked up with red, tearful eyes and said, "Yes it was, and you're right he could not get off the stuff."

The lad then said, *'Tell Jordan I love him and I am here most of the time. I watch her bath him and woke her up last night when he had a temperature.'*

I again relayed all this to which the young lady answered, "You are so right, but I miss him so much."

With that the young man pulled away. I sat back and felt the energy of the link slowly lift, that was it. The young lady ran up and gave me a peck on the cheek, she said, "You would never have known all that, I know he is around now," and looking down at the tape in her hand she said, partly to herself, "I will always love him." With that, my job done, I headed for my car.

In November of 2006 a friend of mine informed me of a television program looking for Psychics to take part in an up and coming television show called 'Britain's Psychic Challenge.'

I checked this out on the computer and found it was by 'Town-House' television company and the show would be on Channel Five, hosted by Trisha Goddard of the 'Trisha' talk show.

I applied, not thinking that I would even get an interview as they had been asking for people to apply for quite a while.

About three days later I received a telephone call asking me to go to Teddington Lock television studios for an interview. On arrival I was ushered into a small area, like a place where business people wait using laptops.

I could tell who had come to the television show interview, it is not hard for one Psychic to know another by their energy or their aura. Finally, a young lady called my name out and I followed her to a small meeting room where I met a lady named Deborah Borgan. Deborah was a Norwegian lady and also a Clairvoyant Medium and Psychic. Deborah had been one of the first Mediums to take part in the television show 'Sensing Murder.'

Deborah was going to be the coach and mentor during the show.

I was then led into a small room with a camera and about four camera and sound people.

Deborah asked me for details about my past performances, the theatres I had demonstrated in: the Alhambra in Bradford, the Marine Hall in Fleetwood, also the Guildhall, Derby and many others. She asked me to describe her home in Norway.

I sat and was immediately aware of a house on a corner with a for sale sign on. It had a very pointed roof, and had a large garden at the front. It was detached, the woodwork was brown and it was an old house. Deborah smiled and said, "Well done Dennis." She then handed me a large A4 brown envelope and asked, "Can you describe the person in here?"

I sat with it for a minute and straight away was aware of her mother.

I said, "This is your mother Deborah." Her eyes lit up.

I then said, "She looks like the Queen Mother."

Deborah clapped her hands and sat back laughing, "Well done again Dennis. Are you free December 2006, January and February of 2007?"

I said, "Well if I have to be, yes I will be." And with that I left.

About a week later I had a gentleman telephone me from the 'Town-House' television company who said, "Well done Dennis. You've been selected as one of the eight to go forward in the television program."

I was amazed and all my family were jumping up

and down. Ev was so pleased.

I was given the dates to go to a hotel near Teddington Lock Studio, just before Christmas. I was to meet up with the other seven Psychics and Deborah to spend a weekend at a boot camp to get to know one another and how we all work.

The date soon came around. I packed my bag, said goodbye to Ev and the children and set off.

On arrival, the first person I met was a guy named Dave Summerton who was also in the Army like me. We got on like a house on fire.

Slowly the other six began drifting into the hotel and we all met in the bar.

There was Dave and me, Diane Lazarus, Mary White, Austin Charles, Anna Galliers, Amanda Hart and Soleira Green. We all got on very well.

We met Deborah who explained what was going to happen during the weekend: the Saturday would be taken up meditating, working Psychically with information hidden in envelopes, (pictures etc.), and working with Psychometry.

This is when a Psychic holds an item which belongs to someone and the Psychic can gain information from the object. This could be many things. It could be about the person who owns the item, the condition the item was in, or something about the house or car.

We had a great Saturday and we were very tired by the evening.

On Sunday, there were challenges that people all

seem to remember the most. This is the one that will always stay with me.

We had just ended doing a challenge at Lincoln jail/castle. We had no idea where we were headed and drove through the night, until we ended up at a public house in the middle of nowhere. We were given a key and taken immediately to our rooms. I unpacked and was aware straight away of movement. Out of the corner of my eye I could see a young girl, aged about six years old, white blonde hair and big blue eyes. She was sitting on a fixture that was no longer there and with her legs crossed she was swinging them and playing with a lock of hair at the side of her head.

As I slowly turned my head I could see she was dirty and her hair matted, but with natural waves. She giggled as she looked at me, and then suddenly a lad, aged a bit older than the girl, appeared.

He had a basic haircut, like a ring of hair had been cut. Many years ago, people used to cut men's and boy's hair by placing a basin over their head and then all the hair outside the basin was shaved away. It looked a bit like a monk's haircut.

He was filthy and had one tooth missing at the front of his mouth. I could smell him. He smelt like earth, he was that dirty. He glared at me with his hands on his hips and stuck his tongue out, so I turned and stuck my tongue out to him and like that they were gone.

I was now nearly ready to climb into bed; it was

not a big room but a very, very old building. The toilet and shower were en-suite and I had a shower. Then, as I was brushing my teeth, I could hear someone knocking the wall behind where the head of my bed was. I thought this was Dave Sumerton having a laugh, so I knocked back and Dave answered again. This went on for a while and I was shouting at the wall, "Get some sleep Sumerton." Finally, I fell asleep.

The next morning I was awakened by a loud knock on the door, I opened it and there was the film crew; the sound guy, directors etc. and there was me in under pants and 'T' shirt.

I said, "You've got to be kidding, this hour of the morning?"

The director said, "What did you see or hear last night?"

"Hang on a minute," I said and quickly put on a dressing gown and sat on the bed.

I explained about the girl and the boy, and then about the knocking from the wall behind the headboard.

I smiled as I said, "I bet Sumerton is behind this wall."

All the windows were locked and the night before it was thick with fog, I knew I was on the ground floor.

The director unlocked the windows and leaning out I looked and there was nothing there. I mean no Inn, it was a graveyard and down to where my headboard would have been was a huge and very old, grey, grave stone.

The crew were taking us all one at a time for a walk through the Inn, as we knew it was by then, and see what we could pick up.

As with all the challenges, when a Psychic has finished his or her challenge they are taken away to another location so no information can be passed on, soon enough it was my turn.

I left the bedroom where I had been all night. Breakfast was brought to the bedrooms, there were no telephones, no televisions and all mobile phones had been collected.

I still didn't know where I was.

At my bedroom door was a camera crew, a sound guy, Jackie Moulton, one of the sceptics that was working on the show, and a historian who knew all sorts of details about this establishment.

As soon as I left the bedroom, I stood still. I saw his face as clear as day.

I was then taken outside where a white van was parked in the car park at the front. I was then shown a tape. I knew who this was. I suddenly stopped in my tracks and said, "Peter Sutcliffe has been here, hasn't he? The serial killer I mean, we must be near to York then."

The historian stepped forward and said, "Stop the filming."

There was a conference going on and then they turned back to me, the director approached me and took me to one side, he looked worried, "Dennis, they won't allow this to be part of the program."

I looked perplexed, and said, "What did they expect having Psychics here?"

"It is one hundred percent right. Sutcliffe was here, but they don't want this establishment to be connected with him."

I complained that this was a vital piece of evidence as to the history of the place. The director just shrugged his shoulders and it was never shown. I carried on with my walk about, somewhat deflated now and was aware of children everywhere and a matronly type figure in period costume surrounded by children. This was confirmed as correct; the upstairs was used as a nursery many years ago.

We had some fun, the other challengers and myself.

"Do not drink too much. Work in the morning," Deborah would say, as we were all in the hotel bar. There are some things I will always remember. Some mornings when we would be getting ready to leave to an undisclosed location, the director would get us all on camera after breakfast every morning, and say, "Okay, anyone got any idea where we are going today?"

We would be filmed and many mornings we would get a hit, like the morning when one of us said, "It feels like a spa, a place of healing."

The director went red in the face, "Who told you that? Who give you that information?" We all stood back shocked, as there was never ever any information given. Everyone was too interested in what we could get right or wrong. One morning we all said "You have a show with Psychics on; you ask questions as to where we are going or the conditions there and when we are right, you throw a fit." He never did it again.

I never noticed, until I got home, that some of the sceptics could be found on sometimes as many as five different channels on Paranormal programmes, working as a Sceptic. Why would they throw their arms in the air and shout, "I believe." What would they do then? Who wants a sceptic that believes?

CHAPTER 22 – Mum

Every New Year's Eve was a nightmare. On New Year's Day, we would wait for 9.15pm to come around and no matter where we were or what we were doing, we would all hold one another for two minutes. If we were at home, we would light a candle.

I was asked to go to the Spiritualist church at Cannock.

As I arrived and was walking towards the church, I wondered if I would be okay, I had never done a service here before and was slightly apprehensive. However, as I opened the door and stepped in I heard a familiar sound playing on their music centre. It was *Tears in heaven.* I thought, 'Wow boy, you certainly know how to give me confidence.'

The service went without a hitch, the evidence was strong, all links taken and many tissues were handed out.

I soon had my diary full of dates for doing services and evenings of Clairvoyance on Fridays, Saturdays and Sundays.

My youngest daughter, Natasha, was now helping me with the administration of dates and places and in 2008 I started a tour of theatres across the UK called 'Voices.'

On 1st July 2009 I received a phone call from my sister, Stella: "Dennis, Mum has had a fall. She is with Barry and they are waiting for an ambulance."

Myself, Evelyn and Natasha raced to Kettering General Hospital. We got there before the ambulance.

I met Mum as she was being wheeled in by the ambulance guys. Barry looked worried, and Mum was frantic. "I am not stopping in bloody hospital. Do you hear?" Mum demanded. I tried to reason with her but she was adamant.

Two doctors arrived; Mum had to have an x-ray as she had already had a fall five years prior and broken her hip and it was the same hip that was now hurting. An x-ray was taken and it was found her hip was fine but her kidneys were in poor condition. After all Mum was ninety -three.

They admitted her and she slowly declined. Her kidneys deteriorated and she had water on her lungs due to this. However, she started to get better and taking more note of what was going on, so on July 12th, Evelyn and myself left for Germany. I was teaching a three-day workshop on Mediumship and an evening of Clairvoyance.

We arrived on the Friday and all went well until 2am, Wednesday morning. I got a telephone call from Natasha, "Dad, come home quick, Nan has had five heart attacks tonight and the staff here don't think she will last much longer."

I was frantic trying to find a flight home and on the Thursday, we flew back to the UK

On the way home, we passed through Kettering and stopped at the hospital; there were nurses and doctors everywhere. A doctor called me to the nurse's station in Mum's ward and explained, "Your mother's kidneys are only working at about two percent and she has a severe chest infection. Plus, with the five heart attacks she has had, it does not look good."

I went to Mum's bed and her breathing was highly erratic. Although she knew I was there she could not talk.

I sat there all night with Evelyn and Natasha, expecting Mum to pass away at every second.

As the dawn came, I sat outside the ward and called in the Angels to help. I asked for Ark Angel Michael to give her strength. Raphael to heal and if not to make my mother better then to help with her transition to the Spirit World. Also, Gabriel I asked to help Mum with all the toxins in her body due to her kidneys not working properly.

I returned to Mum's bedside, her breathing was laborious and still erratic but she had made it through the night. We had to go home to shower and change and make sure the house was okay.

HEAVEN'S MESSENGER

We returned later in the day.

Mum and me

Mum was struggling and her doctor said, "If anyone has not seen your mother and they wish to, now is the time."

I returned to Mum's bedside and she was whispering. I could not hear her so I bent my ear to her mouth and she whispered, "How long?"

I said, "What?"

She replied in a whisper, hardly audible, "How long have I got?"

I tried not to let her see my tears, I said, "You're going nowhere. Is it worth fighting for?"

Mum whispered, "What?" in-between fighting for her breath.

I said again, "Mum, is life worth fighting for?"

Mum nodded. I said, "If you don't quit I won't quit. Okay?"

She smiled and nodded again. By then my two daughters, Craig and my son-in-law, Michael, had arrived.

I took a walk with Evelyn and had a coffee and when we returned they had gone.
I sat with Mum all afternoon and again she was trying to say something. I bent to hear what she was saying. She asked what the music was. I listened, and sure enough I could hear music from the next ward and as I listened the beautiful sound of that lovely song *In the arms of an Angel* by Sarah McLaughlin wafted through the ward.
I asked the nurse where the music was coming from and she replied that they had a radio on in the next ward.
Mum said, "Listen to the Angel music Dennis, you're Heaven's messenger son." I could not help crying.

Thursday night came and again Evelyn and myself sat with Mum until two in the morning. When the nurse explained that her stats, (blood, oxygen etc.) where settling down and they would need our telephone number, just in case, I kissed Mum and we went home and got into bed. I was asleep in a second.
On the Friday, we returned to the hospital arriving at about 9am. We had had no breakfast, not even a coffee.

I saw the doctor with Mum and waited until he had finished then I asked how she was doing, he replied, "I don't understand. By all accounts she should not be here. She is still seriously ill and we could lose her in the next heart beat but for now, she remains the same."
I was elated by the news, "Let's go for breakie," I said to Evelyn.
Off we went, I stood in the queue of the WRVS shop and from the back room I could hear music again and once more the song, *In the arms of an Angel* was being sung. I smiled to myself and whispered a heartfelt 'Thank you.'
Mum got stronger and stronger, although her care needs now were so reliant on twenty-four-hour care. She had to go into a nursing home and I would collect her three to four times a week, and through the warm days of late May and June she would sit outside my front door, watching all the neighbours and children playing. They all got to know Mum and she would natter for hours.

It was about 8.30am on July 17th; I was up and sorting papers out for a theatre, when the telephone rang. Evelyn answered it and said, "It's for you."
"Hello?
My sister said, "Are you sitting down?" I knew.
"We lost Mum at seven-thirty this morning".
I don't remember much after that. I rang the care home and asked if I could see Mum and they said

yes. Natasha wanted to come to see her nan, so we both set off for the care home. I remember walking in and Mum laid there just as if she was asleep, I held her hand and she was still warm, so I kissed her on the forehead and said, "Sweet dreams Ma." A nurse came in and explained, "Your mum woke about seven-fifteen this morning, so I made her a cup of tea and put her television on. She was talking to me about Michael Jackson, when I noticed a couple of her towels were a bit grubby, so I said, 'I will change these for you Audrey' and I only went next door where housekeeping is, placed two towels in a laundry bag and fetched two clean ones. Your Mum had passed away inside a minute."
That is how I prayed for Mum to go, no pain, no fear, be gentle and make it quick.

Mum's funeral was on July 25th and we had 'In the arms of an Angel' played. An end of an era had come to pass, Mum was the last of a long line of characters, the like we will never see again.

I was aware of my Clair's of Clairvoyance, Clairaudiance and Clairsentience but also, I was picking up Clairoma. I would be aware of after shaves, like Old Spice, cigar or cigarette smoke. I knew what a rose smelt like, lavender and 'Chanel No 5.' A Clairknowing is when you just 'know' something, no reason, no visions or talking, it is just there in your head and not Psychic. What is the difference between Psychic knowledge and Spiritual knowledge as we receive it?

Psychic is when you are dealing with materialistic things, like the washing machine is broken. To me it feels cold, like one to one. I put it like throwing my Aura over the other person's Aura and you receive information about that person. Spiritual, now I can only tell you how it is with me.

I must place my head in the old comfortable place, it feels lighter, the information, and of course I am aware of the source when someone from the Spirit World is with me. I found that this can be as complicated or as easy as we want it to be; I have heard many things now that fly over the top of my head.

I smile to myself as I hear someone complicate the simplest of things to make it seem more important than it is, or make themselves more important.

By now I was working regularly in Spiritual Churches as far as Oxford and London. I wanted to give better evidence and would meditate the same time and in the same place every day. I became known as Heaven's Messenger due to the accuracy of the messenger.

I now travel to Dubai, Germany, Gibraltar, Spain and USA to teach and demonstrate my ability. Many, many more strange things have happened. But that is for later.

If that's the first sixty-nine years of my life, I can't wait for the rest.

CHAPTER 23 – Final Thoughts

Here are some poems that I love, to those of you who have lost a loved one. I hope these words heal a little.

Welcome Home:

To those I love and those who love me,
When I am gone, release me.
Let me go,
I have so many things to see and do.

You mustn't tie yourself to me with tears,
Be happy that we had so many years.
I gave you my love, you can only guess,
How much you gave to me in happiness.

I thank you for the love you each have shown,
But now it's time I travelled on alone,
So, grieve a while for me, if grieve you must,
Then let your grief be comforted by trust.

It's only for a while that we must part,

HEAVEN'S MESSENGER

So bless the memories within your heart.
I won't be far away, for life goes on,
For if you need me, call and I will come.

Though you can't see or touch me, I'll be near,
And if you listen with your heart you'll hear,
All of my love around you,
Soft and clear.

And then,
When you must come this way alone,
I'll greet you with a smile
And 'Welcome Home.'

God's Garden:

God looked around his garden
And He found an empty place.
And then He looked down upon the earth,
and saw your tired face.

He put His arms around you,
And lifted you to rest.
God's garden must be beautiful,
He always takes the best.

He knew that you were suffering,
He knew you were in pain,
He knew that you would never,
Get well on earth again.
He saw the road was getting rough,

HEAVEN'S MESSENGER

And the hills were hard to climb,
So He closed your weary eyelids,
And whispered "Peace be thine."

It broke our hearts to lose you.
But you didn't go alone,
for part of us went with you,
The day God that called you home.

You Can Let Me Go:

We've known lots of pleasure,
At times, endured pain,
We've lived in the sunshine
And walked in the rain.

But now we're separated
And for a time apart,
But I am not alone,
Forever you're in my heart.

Death always seems so sudden,
And it is always sure,
But what is oft' forgotten,
It is not without a cure.

There may be times you miss me,
I sort of hope you do,
But smile when you think of me,
For I'll be waiting for you.
Now there's many things for you to do,

And lots of ways to grow,
So, get busy, be happy, and live your life,
Miss me, but let me go.

Namaste

God bless

My website is http://clairvoyantandpsychic.com

Hayley, Craig, me, Scott and Natasha